Parenting Hyperactive Preschoolers

 **PROGRAMS** THAT WORK

Parenting Hyperactive Preschoolers

CLINICIAN GUIDE

ELIZABETH A. HARVEY

SHARONNE D. HERBERT

REBECCA M. STOWE

OXFORD

UNIVERSITY PRESS

OXFORD
UNIVERSITY PRESS

Oxford University Press is a department of the University of
Oxford. It furthers the University's objective of excellence in research,
scholarship, and education by publishing worldwide.

Oxford   New York
Auckland   Cape Town   Dar es Salaam   Hong Kong   Karachi
Kuala Lumpur   Madrid   Melbourne   Mexico City   Nairobi
New Delhi   Shanghai   Taipei   Toronto

With offices in
Argentina   Austria   Brazil   Chile   Czech Republic   France   Greece
Guatemala   Hungary   Italy   Japan   Poland   Portugal   Singapore
South Korea   Switzerland   Thailand   Turkey   Ukraine   Vietnam

Oxford is a registered trademark of Oxford University Press
in the UK and certain other countries.

Published in the United States of America by
Oxford University Press
198 Madison Avenue, New York, NY 10016

Library of Congress Cataloging-in-Publication Data
Harvey, Elizabeth A. (Psychologist)
Parenting hyperactive preschoolers : clinician guide / Elizabeth A. Harvey, Sharonne D. Herbert, Rebecca M. Stowe.
pages cm.—(Programs that work)
Includes bibliographical references.
ISBN 978–0–19–020463–1 (alk. paper)
1. Hyperactive children—Behavior modification.   2. Parents of attention-deficit-disordered children.
3. Preschool children.   I. Title.
RJ506.H9H3856 2015
371.94—dc23
2014044318

9 8 7 6 5 4 3 2 1
Printed in the United States of America
on acid-free paper

Stunning developments in healthcare have taken place over the last several years, but many of our widely accepted interventions and strategies in mental health and behavioral medicine have been brought into question by research evidence as not only lacking benefit but also, perhaps, inducing harm (Barlow, 2010). Other strategies have been proven effective using the best current standards of evidence, resulting in broad-based recommendations to make these practices more available to the public (McHugh & Barlow, 2010). Several recent developments are behind this revolution. First, we have arrived at a much deeper understanding of pathology, both psychological and physical, which has led to the development of new, more precisely targeted interventions. Second, our research methodologies have improved substantially, such that we have reduced threats to internal and external validity, making the outcomes more directly applicable to clinical situations. Third, governments around the world and healthcare systems and policymakers have decided that the quality of care should improve, that it should be evidence based, and that it is in the public's interest to ensure that this happens (Barlow, 2004; Institute of Medicine, 2001; McHugh & Barlow, 2010).

Of course, the major stumbling block for clinicians everywhere is the accessibility of newly developed evidence-based psychological interventions. Workshops and books can go only so far in acquainting responsible and conscientious practitioners with the latest behavioral healthcare practices and their applicability to individual patients. This new series, Programs*ThatWork*, is devoted to communicating these exciting new interventions to clinicians on the frontlines of practice.

The manuals and workbooks in this series contain step-by-step detailed procedures for assessing and treating specific problems and diagnoses. But this series also goes beyond the books and manuals by providing ancillary materials that will approximate the supervisory process in assisting practitioners in the implementation of these procedures in their practice.

In our emerging healthcare system, the growing consensus is that evidence-based practice offers the most responsible course of action for the mental health professional. All behavioral healthcare clinicians deeply desire to provide the best possible care for their patients. In this series, our aim is to close the dissemination and information gap and make that possible.

This therapist guide addresses the challenge of parenting hyperactive preschoolers. Parenting a young child who exhibits extreme hyperactivity and impulsivity can prove to be very difficult, requiring extra patience, effort, and skill. Additionally, children with symptoms of attention deficit hyperactivity disorder (ADHD) can have substantial difficulties with emotion regulation and are at risk for developing emotional or behavioral disorders, so the problem is one of great importance and common concern among families.

The program presented in this therapist guide outlines a 14-week parent training and emotion socialization program designed to be delivered in 90-minute sessions, in either a group or individual setting. It guides clinicians in providing parents with needed tools to help their hyperactive children to behave in adaptive, socially appropriate ways that will also help prevent their children from developing further difficulties. The treatment focuses on behavior management strategies tailored for children with hyperactive symptoms and teaches parents emotion socialization skills that are linked to better emotion regulation in children. The manual also includes homework forms and handouts for parents and children to help guide them in applying their newly learned skills at home.

David H. Barlow, Editor-in-Chief,
Programs *ThatWork*
Boston, MA

References

Barlow, D.H. (2004). Psychological treatments. *American Psychologist, 59*, 869–878.

Barlow, D.H. (2010). Negative effects from psychological treatments: A perspective. *American Psychologist, 65*(2), 13–20.

Institute of Medicine. (2001). *Crossing the quality chasm: A new health system for the 21st century.* Washington, DC: National Academy Press.

McHugh, R.K., & Barlow, D.H. (2010). Dissemination and implementation of evidence-based psychological interventions: A review of current efforts. *American Psychologist, 65*(2), 73–84.

Contents

Acknowledgments

We would like to acknowledge the many people who have influenced our thinking about this program, including our mentors and colleagues, many influential experts in the field of parenting and ADHD, and our own parents and children. We would also like to thank the clinicians and families who were involved in the first parenting groups using an earlier draft of this program and who helped us in refining it. Finally, we would like to thank the UMass Psychological Services Center, which provided support during the development of this program.

Parenting Hyperactive Preschoolers

CHAPTER 1

Introductory Information for Clinicians

Background Information and Purpose of This Program

The goal of this program is to provide parents[1] with a set of tools to better manage preschoolers who are extremely active and impulsive. Parenting any preschooler can be challenging, but when hyperactivity and impulsivity are extreme, parenting requires extraordinary effort and skill. Parents need tools not only for helping their children to behave in ways that are adaptive and socially appropriate, but also for preventing their children from developing additional difficulties. Children who are hyperactive are at risk for developing emotional or behavioral disorders (Barkley, 2006), and family interactions during the preschool years may play a key role in this process. Because parenting hyperactive preschoolers can be very stressful, it can be easy to fall into interaction patterns that make a difficult situation even worse. For example, a coercive cycle (Patterson, 2002) can develop, in which difficult child behaviors elicit harsh parenting practices, which in turn not only exacerbate the difficult child behaviors but also may sow the seeds for additional emotional and behavior problems. By intervening early, we hope to interrupt this cycle, reduce the difficult child behaviors, and prevent the development of additional difficulties.

This program consists of 14 sessions, which focus on teaching parenting strategies for managing hyperactive and oppositional behavior and

---

[1] We use the term *parents* for convenience, but include any adult who provides a significant caregiving role for the child. This may include guardians, grandparents, aunts and uncles, or parents' partners.

for helping children develop better emotion regulation. Sessions last approximately 1½ hours and are designed to be conducted in a group setting, which allows parents to receive support and input from each other. However, the program can be easily adapted to individual sessions, which can be shorter because there is less discussion than in a group. This program is designed to be used by clinicians who have had graduate training in child mental health, including education on parenting and child development.

Disorder or Problem Focus

This program is designed for hyperactive preschoolers, many of whom have or are at risk for developing attention deficit hyperactivity disorder (ADHD). (See *DSM-5* for criteria for ADHD; American Psychiatric Association, 2013.) Preschoolers are typically active and high in energy. This is part of normal development and not a cause for concern. Why then do we need to provide guidance for parents of hyperactive preschoolers? It turns out that there is an important difference between preschoolers who are extremely active—whose activity level and impulsivity is much higher than that of most other preschoolers—and preschoolers who show levels of hyperactivity that are average or even somewhat above average for their age. Unlike typically active preschoolers who are likely to outgrow these behaviors, preschoolers who are extremely active—for example, more active than 95% of their peers—are likely to continue to have difficulties with hyperactivity as they grow older. It is estimated that between 75% and 90% of preschoolers with clinically significant levels of hyperactivity will meet criteria for ADHD during their school-age years (Harvey, Youngwirth, Thakar, & Errazuriz, 2009; Lahey, Pelham, Loney, Lee, & Willcutt, 2005; Riddle et al., 2013). Moreover, ADHD is common among preschoolers, with an estimated 4.2% of them meeting criteria for ADHD (Egger, Kondo, & Angold, 2006). Thus, although in the past it has been common for healthcare professionals to take a wait-and-see approach with hyperactive preschoolers (Fanton, MacDonald, & Harvey, 2008), there is growing evidence that early intervention may be appropriate. Early intervention may be particularly effective for young children whose brains are rapidly developing and are therefore potentially more receptive to being rewired based on experiences (Nelson & Bloom, 1997).

There has been a growing recognition over the past decade that ADHD often begins during the preschool years. In 2011, guidelines for diagnosing ADHD were expanded by the American Academy of Pediatrics (AAP) to include children as young as 4 years of age (Subcommittee on Attention-Deficit/Hyperactivity Disorder Committee on Quality, 2011). However, a relatively small proportion of children are diagnosed with ADHD during the preschool years. In 2012, The Centers for Disease Control reported that 1.7% of 3- to 4-year-old children had been diagnosed with ADHD, compared to 9.5% of 5- to 11-year-old children (Bloom, Cohen, & Freeman, 2012). Thus, it is important to provide interventions not only for preschoolers who have been diagnosed with ADHD, but also for preschoolers exhibiting early signs of ADHD who may not yet have been diagnosed. Parents may ask whether they should have their children evaluated for ADHD, and appropriate referral information should be provided to parents who inquire. However, it should be emphasized to parents that a diagnosis of ADHD is not required for children to benefit from this program.

Development of This Treatment Program and Evidence Base

With mounting evidence that ADHD often begins during the preschool years, there has been a growing recognition of the need to develop and evaluate interventions for preschoolers with or at risk for ADHD. This led to the launching of a large randomized controlled trial to examine the efficacy of psychopharmacological interventions for preschoolers, the Preschoolers with Attention-Deficit/Hyperactivity Disorder Treatment Study (PATS; Kollins et al., 2006). Although the PATS found some evidence that stimulant medication is efficacious in this age group, effect sizes appear to be lower for preschool-aged children than for school-aged children (Greenhill et al., 2006). Moreover, psychopharmacological treatment in preschool-aged children has been associated with declines in growth rates (Swanson et al., 2007), moderate to severe adverse events (e.g., emotional outbursts, difficulty falling asleep, repetitive behavior/thoughts, decreased appetite) in almost one-third of preschoolers (Wigal et al., 2006), and much higher rates of children discontinuing medication (11% in PATS) compared to school-aged children (less than 1% in the Multimodal Treatment of ADHD study; Wigal et al., 2006). These results, coupled with the fact that little is known about the long-term effects of medication on brain development in young children, highlight the need to develop alternatives to drug therapy.

Evidence Supporting the Use of Parent Training

The AAP recommends that behavioral treatments such as parent training should be the first line of treatment for preschoolers with ADHD (Subcommittee on Attention-Deficit/Hyperactivity Disorder Committee on Quality, 2011). Parent training programs have long been shown to be effective treatments for preschool-aged children with conduct and oppositional problems (e.g., Reid, Webster-Stratton, & Baydar, 2004) and have also been used to treat school-aged children with ADHD (Barkley, 2013; Danforth, Harvey, Ulaszek, & McKee, 2006). A smaller but growing body of research has evaluated the effectiveness of parent training for preschool-aged children with significant ADHD symptoms. Several randomized controlled trials of preschoolers with symptoms of ADHD have found significant reductions in ADHD symptoms (Jones, Daley, Hutchings, Bywater, & Eames, 2008; Matos, Bauermeister, & Bernal, 2009; Sonuga-Barke, Daley, Thompson, Laver-Bradbury, & Weeks, 2001; Strayhorn & Weidman, 1989; Thompson et al., 2009; Webster-Stratton, Reid, & Beauchaine, 2011) or associated behavior problems (Bor, Sanders, & Markie-Dadds, 2002; Pisterman et al., 1992; Pisterman, McGrath, Firestone, & Goodman, 1989) following parent training compared to a control group. Follow-up studies have also documented improvement as much as 18 months post-treatment (Bor et al., 2002; Jones et al., 2008; Pisterman et al., 1992, 1989; Strayhorn & Weidman, 1991). Additional studies without a no-treatment control group have reported significant changes in ADHD symptoms from pre-treatment to post-treatment (DuPaul & Kern, 2013; Huang, Chao, Tu, & Yang, 2003; Kern et al., 2007).

Parent training programs that have been used for hyperactive preschoolers are grounded in a large base of theory and research that point to parenting practices that are most effective in fostering healthy child development. These programs are guided by a number of theoretical frameworks. Many programs are largely based on social learning theory, which holds that behavior is learned and changed through social interactions (Bandura, 1978). Some programs (e.g., Parent-Child Interaction Therapy; Eyberg & Bussing, 2010) are also grounded in attachment theory (Bowlby, 1983). Guided by these theories, strategies are designed to increase positive parent–child interactions and reinforce positive behavior and typically teach parents to use effective commands, tangible rewards, and appropriate consequences (e.g., Bor et al., 2002; Huang et al., 2003; Kern et al., 2007; Pisterman et al., 1992; Strayhorn & Weidman, 1989). The use of these strategies is supported not only by existing theory but also by a large base of empirical support, which we review in the introductory sections for each session.

Development of the Parenting Hyperactive Preschoolers Program

Parenting Hyperactive Preschoolers was developed specifically for hyperactive preschoolers and therefore places special emphasis on adapting these parenting tools for this population. In addition, because there is growing evidence that children with ADHD tend to have difficulties controlling their emotions (Martel, 2009), this program also has a special emphasis on emotion socialization tools that theory and research suggest are critical for the development of children's emotion regulation (Denham, Bassett, & Wyatt, 2008). In particular, emotion socialization theory (Eisenberg, Cumberland, & Spinrad, 1998) suggests that parents' expression of emotion, discussion of emotion, and reactions to children's emotion are key in shaping the development of children's emotion competence. The focus of this program on emotion socialization is particularly important because the preschool years are thought to be a critical time for emotional development (Supplee, Skuban, Trentacosta, Shaw, & Stoltz, 2011).

The efficacy of this program has recently been evaluated using a randomized controlled trial (Herbert, Harvey, Roberts, Wichowski, & Lugo-Candelas, 2013) with preschool children who demonstrated clinically significant levels of hyperactivity based on a diagnostic interview and/or behavior rating scale. The parenting program was delivered to 17 families in small groups (between 3 and 6 families per group) by clinicians (clinical psychology doctoral students, a school psychologist, and a licensed clinical psychologist) in an outpatient training clinic. Significant and large-sized decreases were found in preschool children's ADHD symptoms (inattention Cohen's $d = .87$; hyperactivity/impulsivity Cohen's $d = .71$), and moderate-sized decreases were reported in children's oppositional defiance (Cohen's $d = .44$) at the end of the parenting program compared to waitlist children. Moderate improvement was also found on one of two subscales measuring emotion regulation (emotional lability; Cohen's $d = .45$) but was not observed on another subscale assessing empathy, emotional self-awareness, and responding positively to others, nor on an observational measure of child misbehavior and negative affect.

Larger scale studies will be needed to replicate these findings, examine whether improvement can be observed outside of the home setting, evaluate the effectiveness of this program outside of a research setting, and examine whether these effects are maintained over time.

What Is Social Learning Theory and Emotion Socialization Theory?

Although ADHD is thought to be caused by biological factors, socialization plays an important role in the way ADHD symptoms manifest themselves and in the development of co-occurring emotional and behavioral problems (Johnston & Mash, 2001). Social learning theory and emotion socialization theory articulate the ways in which parenting may shape children's behavioral and emotional development.

Social learning theory (see Figure 1.1) argues that behavior, internal processes (e.g., thoughts), and the environment influence one another in a dynamic and reciprocal manner (Bandura, 1978). Principles of reinforcement and punishment (Skinner, 1974) are integrated in this theory, and are important mechanisms through which these domains affect one another. Thus, social learning theory argues that behavior is shaped by its consequences, and these consequences may be external (e.g., a parent rewarding or punishing a child), internal (e.g., positive emotions or thoughts), or both. Moreover, behavior, in turn, influences both internal experiences and the environment. Thus, social learning theory emphasizes the importance of parenting in young children's development but recognizes the complex ways in which parents and children influence one another and highlights the important role that children's internal processes play in guiding and motivating their behavior.

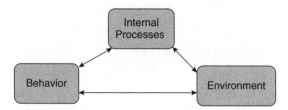

Figure 1.1

Social Learning Theory Model
Adapted from Bandura, A. (1978). The self system in reciprocal determinism. *American Psychologist, 33*(4), 344–358.

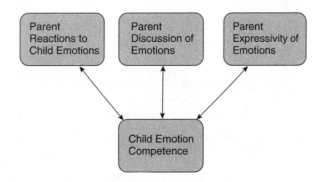

Figure 1.2

Emotion Socialization Model
Figure created based on text from Eisenberg, N., Cumberland, A., & Spinrad, T. L.
(1998). Parental socialization of emotion. *Psychological Inquiry, 9*(4), 241–273.

Emotion socialization theory (Eisenberg et al., 1998) suggests that parents play a critical role in the development of children's emotion competence, including children's understanding of emotion, expression of emotion, and ability to regulate emotions. In particular, parents' reactions to emotions, discussion of emotions, and expressivity of emotions all contribute to the development of children's emotion competence, which in turn lays an important foundation for their social and emotional functioning (see Figure 1.2). Parents who are sensitive to and supportive of children's emotional experience, model appropriate expression of emotion, and talk with and educate their children about emotion tend to have children who are more emotionally competent (Eisenberg et al., 1998).

Risks and Benefits of This Treatment Program

When successfully implemented, this program has the potential to foster positive parent–child relationships and to support children's behavioral and emotional functioning. It is, however, important for leaders to be aware of potential pitfalls.

First, parents come to treatment with a variety of different beliefs about parenting. It is critical to be respectful of parents and their views and to avoid judging them. The parenthood status of group leaders can further complicate this issue. Group leaders who are not parents themselves may have difficulty fully understanding the experiences of parents. At the same time, group leaders who are parents may have their own well-established beliefs about parenting, and it may be difficult not to try to impose these on parents in the group. The goal of the leaders is to help parents determine how to best use the strategies in the program within the context of parents' own value systems.

Similarly, the strategies in this program can be difficult to implement, and no parent can do so perfectly. It is critical to create a safe atmosphere in which parents feel comfortable being imperfect. This means that when parents describe instances in which they are using parenting practices that may not be ideal, it is important for them to not feel judged. For example, if parents describe losing their temper with their children, it would be better to empathize with how difficult it can be to stay calm than to lecture the parents about not yelling.

Alternative Treatments

Behavioral parent training is considered the first line of treatment for hyperactive preschoolers (Rajwan, Chacko, & Moeller, 2012; Subcommittee on Attention-Deficit/Hyperactivity Disorder Committee on Quality, 2011). A number of other parenting programs have been demonstrated to be efficacious in helping hyperactive preschoolers, including the Incredible Years Program (Webster-Stratton et al., 2011), Triple P Positive Parenting Program (Bor et al., 2002), and Parent-Child Interaction Therapy (Matos et al., 2009). Stimulant medication has also demonstrated effectiveness in the management of ADHD in preschoolers (Greenhill et al., 2006), although more side effects have been reported in preschoolers than in older children (Wigal et al., 2006).

The Role of Medications

For school-aged children with ADHD, the AAP recommends stimulant medication, which has been widely documented to reduce ADHD symptomatology in older children. However, for preschoolers with ADHD, the AAP recommends behavior therapy (e.g., parent or teacher training) as the first line of treatment and recommends medication only for children who do not respond to such intervention

(Subcommittee on Attention-Deficit/Hyperactivity Disorder Committee on Quality, 2011). Although no studies have directly compared the effectiveness of parent management training and medication for preschoolers with ADHD, cross-study comparisons suggest that parent management training is at least as efficacious, if not more so, than stimulant medication (Greenhill et al., 2006; Herbert et al., 2013; Jones et al., 2008; Matos et al., 2009; Sonuga-Barke et al., 2001; Strayhorn & Weidman, 1989; Thompson et al., 2009; Webster-Stratton et al., 2011). Nonetheless, stimulant medication use has increased over the past few decades among preschoolers (Visser et al., 2014; Zito et al., 2000) and in 2011 more than half of 4- and 5-year-old children who carried an ADHD diagnosis were reported to be taking medication for ADHD (Visser et al., 2014). Thus, many families who enroll in this program are likely to have children who are taking medication. Although there are currently no studies examining the effectiveness of combining stimulant medication and parent training for preschoolers with ADHD, research with older children suggests that the two treatments are likely to complement one another (The MTA Cooperative Group, 1999). Particularly for children with severe ADHD, the decrease in ADHD symptoms resulting from stimulant medication may make it easier for parents to carry out the strategies in this program. In fact, there is evidence that parents interact quite differently with their children when children are on medication than when they are off medication (Danforth, Barkley, & Stokes, 1991). Because stimulant medication is short-acting and might not be given to young children during the weekends, this program may be particularly useful to parents to help manage behavior during evenings and weekends when children may be less likely to have therapeutic doses of medication in their systems.

Outline of This Treatment Program

This program has two components. The first eight sessions focus on teaching parenting strategies that have been shown to be effective in managing hyperactive and oppositional behavior. The last six sessions focus on teaching parents strategies for helping their children develop better emotion regulation. Table 1.1 provides an overview of the content of each session.

Table 1.1 Session Content

Session	Content
1. Introduction and Managing Hyperactive Behavior	Group leaders educate parents about hyperactivity in preschoolers and provide techniques for channeling hyperactive behavior. Developmental considerations are also introduced.
2. Using Praise Effectively	Group leaders discuss general parenting values and beliefs, learning principles, the importance of praise, and how to use praise effectively.
3. Increasing Positive Interactions and Using Attention to Shape Children's Behavior	Parents learn how to use attention to increase positive interactions with their children and reward positive behavior, as well as how to use ignoring to discourage inappropriate behavior.
4. Setting Up an Effective Reward System	Parents learn how to set up an effective reward system.
5. Using Commands to Guide Children's Behavior	Group leaders discuss ways of talking to children that will make it more likely that children will comply.
6. Using Logical and Natural Consequences and Rewards	Parents learn effective ways of using consequences to discourage inappropriate behavior and rewards to encourage appropriate behavior.
7. Using Time Out	Group leaders review a time out procedure step-by-step and discuss ways in which time out may need to be modified for hyperactive preschoolers.
8. Teaching Children Problem Solving and Negotiating Skills	Parents learn techniques for problem solving with their children as well as encouraging appropriate negotiation skills.
9. Learning About Emotion Development	Group leaders provide families with psychoeducation about emotion regulation in young children.
10. Teaching Children to Identify and Label Emotions	Parents learn how to help children identify and label emotions. Parents teach these skills by labeling emotions as they occur in their children, in themselves, and in others.
11. Handling Children's Negative Emotion — Part One	Parents learn techniques for validating children's emotions and for helping children calm down.
12. Handling Children's Negative Emotion — Part Two	Parents learn how to handle children's negative emotion in the context of co-occurring misbehavior.
13. Giving Children Opportunities to Experience Positive Emotion	Parents learn about ways of fostering positive emotions in children.
14. Modeling Emotion Regulation and Expression	Group leaders discuss the importance of teaching children to regulate their own emotions through parental modeling of emotion regulation.

Use of the Client Handouts

At the end of this book are handouts corresponding with each session; these may be photocopied and given to parents. We encourage group leaders to give relevant handouts to parents at the beginning of each session so that they can make notes as the group discusses each topic. Some of the handouts have exercises that can be done in session, and some are designed to be taken home for homework that is reviewed at the beginning of the subsequent session. Other handouts highlight information that is covered during the session to help parents remember key points. It may be helpful to provide each parent with a three-ring binder and provide them with hole-punched copies of the handouts so that they can add handouts as they go through the program. They can then refer back to material covered in previous sessions, and by the end of the program they will have a workbook that they can use in the future.

Culture and Parenting

Experts in child development have long recognized the importance of the larger cultural context in which parenting occurs (Darling & Steinberg, 1993). By *culture*, we are referring to values and standards of behavior that are shared among a social group that might be defined by, but not limited to, race/ethnicity, social class, gender, religion and/or spirituality, sexual orientation, and geography. As a group leader, it is important to recognize the impact that culture may have on parenting while also recognizing the rich variability within cultures. It is critical not to make assumptions about parents' values and practices based on their cultural background but to be respectful of individual differences in parenting, whether they are a function of differences in culture or simply differences unique to each individual. It may be helpful to think about some of the ways in which parents' values and practices may differ:

- Degree of parental control

- Degree of limit setting

- Use of punitive parenting practices

- Beliefs about spanking

- Importance of teaching children respect for authority

- Familial hierarchy

- Emphasis on the individual versus community/family

- The ways in which emotion is expressed in the family

It is important to validate parents' values while at the same time encouraging them to challenge some of their own assumptions about parenting. Leaders should help parents discover how to use the parenting techniques in this program in a way that fits with their own parenting values. For example, some parents may set strict limits, whereas others might set fewer limits. The techniques in this program teach parents how to enforce the limits that they do set but allow parents to decide what rules to set.

There may, however, be times when the strategies taught in the program directly conflict with a parent's values, and these situations require great clinical skill. For example, a parent may be philosophically opposed to the use of time out. Or, parents may believe that praise might spoil the child or fail to teach the child respect for authority. It is important to approach the situation with an open mind, and strike a balance between adapting the program to fit parents' values and gently challenging parents' assumptions when appropriate. It is critical for group leaders to not be dogmatic and to recognize that, as a group leaders, they have their own parenting values (regardless of their parental status) that can at times make it difficult to take the perspective of parents whose values differ from their own.

Inquiring about parenting practices, values, and styles early in the program is likely to assist clinicians in teaching parents behavioral principles in a culturally sensitive way. For example, clinicians who are aware that a family values religiosity and spirituality, extended family support, and strict discipline can apply this knowledge throughout the program. Framing differences in discipline as dilemmas of coexisting cultural meanings provides parents with the opportunity to compare discipline practices and informs parents about alternative choices for discipline. This approach reduces the likelihood that parents will feel that their cultural parenting practices are being devalued, and promotes understanding and incorporation of alternative and effective parenting practices. Consideration of cultural practices may strengthen the therapeutic alliance and lead to a more positive outcome.

CHAPTER 2

Group Logistics

Forming a Group

Recruitment and Assessment

Parents are often eager for help in managing their hyperactive preschoolers, so it is not usually difficult to find parents who are interested in participating. Informing pediatricians, local mental health providers, and preschools about the availability of the program is often all that is needed to fill a group. We recommend gathering preliminary information from parents by phone before enrolling them in the group to be sure that the program is appropriate for them. Administering a structured or semistructured interview, such as the Kiddie-Disruptive Behavior Disorder Schedule (Keenan, Wakschlag, & Danis, 2001), to assess ADHD symptoms can help ensure that the child is in fact exhibiting clinically significant levels of hyperactivity. A very brief interview regarding the child's medical and psychiatric history can also be useful. Children with particularly complicated physical or mental health issues may benefit instead from individual rather than group services.

Children's Ages

This program is appropriate for children between the ages of 2 years 6 months and 6 years. Although there can be enormous differences between younger preschoolers and older preschoolers, the program discusses how strategies can be adjusted for younger versus older children. There are some advantages to having a more homogeneous age group (for example, just 5- and 6-year-olds); however, we have found that having parents of children of different ages can often enhance parents' learning from each other. Parents of younger children can learn how things might change as their children develop and can learn from more experienced parents.

Providing Childcare

It is ideal if all parents can attend each session, and it can be helpful to have grandparents attend if they are actively involved in the child's life. For this reason, providing onsite childcare can be critical. Parents of hyperactive preschoolers often have a very difficult time finding childcare, and this can be an enormous barrier to attending the program. Without childcare, two-parent families will often have one parent stay home, and single parents may not be able to come at all.

Group Size

Ideal group sizes are between three and six families, although this program can be adapted to be administered individually. It is important to have enough families present so that parents have the opportunity to receive support and learn from each other, but if there are too many families it can be difficult to have enough time during sessions to check in with each family about their progress. For larger groups, it is typically useful to divide into smaller groups for many of the exercises. We recommend having at least two group leaders, particularly for larger groups, to facilitate activities in which parents divide into smaller groups. Having two group leaders can also be useful in helping manage any difficult group dynamics that may arise.

Group Meetings and Program Duration

This program consists of 14 sessions, each lasting approximately 1½ hours, though sessions may be somewhat longer for larger groups. We recommend meeting weekly so that parents have time to practice the strategies between each session, but do not have to wait long for the next session if they are having difficulty with the strategies.

Ordering of Sessions

Although there may be some flexibility in the order in which sessions are administered, the sequence was designed to begin by laying a positive foundation before introducing limit setting, because it is thought that limit setting may be more effective in the context of a warm and supportive relationship. It is also important for parents to have solid behavior-management skills before tackling emotion socialization. Although it can sometimes be difficult for parents to wait to discuss handling children's emotional outbursts, negative emotions very often occur in the context of misbehavior, so parents must first have a clear understanding of how to manage the misbehavior that is likely to accompany outbursts. Because sessions build on one another, it is also important to help any parent who misses a session "catch up." This can often be done in a shorter amount of time (20 to 30 minutes) on an individual basis, perhaps just before or just after the next session that they attend.

Maintenance or Follow-Up Sessions

Scheduling individual or group booster sessions in the months following the program can be helpful for reinforcing strategies and troubleshooting. These sessions can involve checking in with each family to determine areas that are going well, as well as ongoing difficulties. If these are conducted in a group format, encourage parents to provide support and guidance to each other, stepping in as needed to facilitate effective use of the strategies. At the end of the program, some families may also need referrals for individual treatment to continue receiving support. Parenting a hyperactive child can be very challenging, and ongoing support is often helpful.

Establishing and Building Rapport with Parents

Creating a bond between the group leaders and parents is essential to the success of the program. Furthermore, the manner in which the material is presented can affect the success or failure of the program. To establish and build rapport with parents while lowering parental resistance, consider using the following:

- Convey empathy to parents regarding their circumstances and efforts.

- Emphasize a collaborative process. Parents are experts on their children; the leaders and parents work together to find strategies that work.

- Be facilitative and supportive.

- Use some of the strategies that we teach parents. Express appreciation when parents engage in discussions and when they use effective parenting strategies.

- Use a Socratic style of teaching; guide parents to the conclusion.

- Engage parents in the material.

- Personalize treatment (individual or group) by reviewing what has transpired over the past week.

- Encourage parents to discuss successes and failures.

Group Rules

It is important in the first session to establish ground rules for the group so that everyone in the group feels comfortable. We recommend presenting and reviewing the following rules, as well as asking participants if they have any additional guidelines they would like to suggest for the group.

1. Confidentiality (group leaders and members)

   It is essential both to emphasize the importance of respecting the privacy of other group members and to acknowledge that group members are not bound to the same obligations for confidentiality as group leaders. Thus, there is no guarantee that what participants share in the group will not be shared outside of the group by other group members. Although parents must be warned of the limits of confidentiality in group settings, it is equally important to encourage group members to maintain other parents' confidences. By appealing to parents' sense of moral standards, group leaders may be able to provide some protection of parents' disclosures. It will be important to continue reminding participants of this issue over time (Herbert, Harvey, & Halgin, 2014).

2. One person talks at a time

   Encourage members to listen to one another and avoid interrupting.

3. Step up, step back

   Encourage members to reflect on their own style of group participation, and adjust accordingly. Group members who tend to talk a great deal during discussions should make an effort to let others have a turn (step back), and group members who tend to be quiet should be encouraged to talk (step up).

4. Respect

Be respectful, even if you disagree with someone's opinion (this includes group members being respectful to their own partners who are attending the group).

Troubleshooting

Providing the program in a group setting has the advantage of allowing parents to provide support for one another, but it can also present challenges. It is important to anticipate some of the common challenges that can arise and be prepared to handle them.

Problem Prevention

Being proactive to prevent problems before they arise is ideal. The discussion in the first session regarding ground rules for the group can prevent a number of common problems. Helping parents understand the importance of these rules for maintaining the comfort of group members can prevent problems such as disrespectful behavior and group members who dominate discussion or interrupt others. Modeling of respectful behavior by group leaders can also set the tone for the group and encourage group members to respect, support, and listen to one another.

Helping Members Adhere to Group Rules

If group members are having difficulty following the ground rules that have been established, it can be helpful to revisit those guidelines with the entire group and to highlight the reasons why these rules are important. If difficulties continue, having a private conversation with group members who are dominating or being disrespectful may be helpful. This can be a difficult conversation, and group leaders will need to use effective communication techniques for this to go well. Use of "I" statements and avoiding accusatory statements will be important. For example, a group leader might say to a group member who dominates conversation, "I really appreciate how actively involved you have been in our group discussions and really value your input. But I have been a little worried that some of the quieter members might be having a difficult time stepping up and sharing their ideas. I wonder if you would be willing to help me encourage others to speak, and perhaps step back a little yourself to make room for them?" If this gentle approach does not meet with success, it may be necessary to have a follow-up conversation that is more direct.

Handling Disagreements

It is also common for parents to disagree with one another or to disagree with group leaders about parenting practices. Differences of opinion arise particularly around strictness and control. Session 2 begins with a discussion of parenting values and beliefs, and this can be a good opportunity to set a tone of respect for differences. Disagreeing about parenting need not be discouraged—what is important is that the disagreement is done with a respectful tone. Modeling and explicitly talking about how parents can disagree with one another respectfully can help parents engage in healthy dialogue.

Discouraging Counterproductive Practices

Although it is important to respect differences in parenting beliefs and values, it can be difficult if a parent recommends a practice that group leaders are concerned might be counterproductive. Clearly, if the practice can be considered abusive, leaders are mandated to file a report with child protective services. However, when practices fall short of being abusive but run counter to the goals of the parenting program, it can be challenging. For example, if a parent recommends telling a child that monsters will come get him if he does not behave and reports how well this worked with her own child, group leaders will want to avoid condoning this practice without putting the parent on the spot. Often other parents will jump in and present reasons why the practice might work in the short run but be harmful in the long run, so the first step is to step back and see if parents can help each other work through the issue. If no parent speaks up, group leaders can ask questions to help parents explore intended and unintended consequences of different practices and can respectfully offer their own perspective.

Balancing Leader Facilitation with Parent Interaction

The role of group leaders is to facilitate parents' understanding and implementation of parenting strategies presented in the program. There is a good deal of material to cover, but it is also important to have the material presented as interactively as possible. Group leaders should strike a balance between presenting material and having the group generate ideas. Discussion questions are suggested throughout the curriculum, but group leaders should feel free to create their own discussion questions as well. It is sometimes helpful to give parents time to think about questions before opening up topics for discussion. For example, a leader might say, "Take a few minutes to think about this question and then we will talk about it as a group," or "You can use paper to jot down your thoughts about this question, and then we will talk about your answers as a group." These techniques can be particularly helpful if the group has several quiet members. Parents can learn a great deal from each other; leaders must leave room for parents to talk with, support, and advise each other. It is important to find the right balance between the leaders talking and parents talking.

Presentation and Ordering of Material

The material in the curriculum is designed to give leaders ideas about how to present material, but material should be presented in a conversational and comfortable style. Suggested scripts are indicated in italics, but these are designed to provide ideas for wording; group leaders should not read the material from the curriculum or handouts to parents. Group leaders should also be mindful of the education level of parents in the group; use language that is accessible to all members of the group, and avoid jargon. Within any given section, it is fine to change the order in which material is presented if it seems to make sense for that particular group. For example, if a parent brings up an issue that comes later in the session, it is fine to change the order in which material is presented so that the issue can be addressed at that moment. Leaders should use judgment about whether other material needs to be presented first. If so, it is also appropriate to let the parent know that this is an important issue and will be discussed in a moment. It is also not uncommon for parents to bring up an issue that is relevant to a later session. In those cases it is typically better to inform the parent that the issue will be addressed later in the program.

Group Leaders Who are Not Parents

If a leader is not a parent, it is important to recognize that there are limits to one's ability to fully understand what it is like to be a parent. At the same time, leaders need to feel confident that they have something to offer and not apologize for not being a parent. Leaders will probably be asked at some point whether or not they are parents, so it may be helpful to address this upfront during the introduction. Here is one example: "I am not a parent myself, and although I have had a lot of experience working with children, being a parent and working with other people's children are different. I do know a lot about what experts in the field have found to be effective with children like yours, but you are the expert on your child. Even if I had children, I would not know what it was like to parent your particular child. So we are going to put together our two areas of expertise—your knowledge about what it is like to parent your child and my knowledge about what other parents have found helpful—to figure out together what strategies make the most sense for your particular family."

Training Group Leaders

At least one group leader should have a graduate degree in a mental health field, with training in child development, developmental psychopathology, and experience in working with families. Group leaders should have received training in ethical issues in working with children and families, including education on reporting suspected child abuse. Ideally, training should involve first observing (live or by videotape) an individual administer the program who is experienced in parent training, and then co-leading a group with a more experienced group leader. Supervisors should observe (live or by videotape) group leaders during each session while they are in training and give feedback regarding adherence to the treatment protocols, as well as feedback on skill in presenting material, guiding discussion, and fostering parents' effective use of the strategies.

Session 1 Notes to Group Leaders

Overview

This first session sets the tone for the program and focuses on helping parents to feel comfortable and laying the groundwork for future sessions. In this session, group leaders will orient members of the group to the program, provide psychoeducation regarding preschool hyperactivity, introduce strategies for managing hyperactive behavior in children, and discuss developmental issues.

Introductions and Group Rules

This session begins with introductions. Group leaders introduce themselves and then invite parents to briefly share their primary concerns about their children, as well as the strengths they see in their children. Next, to help foster a positive group dynamic, engage parents in a discussion of expectations regarding participation in the group. Emphasize the importance of respecting other group members' privacy by keeping other participants' contributions in confidence. Explain that although fellow group members are not legally bound to maintain confidentiality, they are strongly encouraged to do so. Make sure that the group members understand the limits of confidentiality, and be sure to review exceptions to confidentiality, such as mandated reporting of child abuse. It is also important to explicitly encourage equal participation from all group members. It can be useful to ask parents to consider whether they tend to speak a great deal in group settings or whether they are more reserved, and to encourage them to adjust their participation levels accordingly.

Psychoeducation on Hyperactivity in Preschoolers and ADHD

Providing parents with information about hyperactivity in preschoolers is also important during the first session, so parents can have a better understanding of their children's behavior before they begin using the program tools. Developmentally, preschoolers are typically active, which can lead to confusion about whether a preschool child's hyperactivity simply reflects a normal developmental stage (Campbell, 2002). In fact, sometimes preschoolers do outgrow their hyperactivity, particularly those whose hyperactivity is less severe (Shaw, Lacourse, & Nagin, 2005). However, there is growing evidence that when preschoolers show clinically significant hyperactivity—that is, hyperactivity that causes significant problems and that is much greater than that of other children of the same age—most will go on to meet criteria for ADHD (Harvey et al., 2009; Lahey et al., 2005; Riddle et al., 2013). Group leaders must strike a balance between acknowledging that preschoolers who are very hyperactive are not likely to outgrow these difficulties and leaving room for the possibility that they might.

This discussion is an important backdrop for providing psychoeducation about ADHD. Group leaders should clarify that information about ADHD is being presented not because children of parents in the group necessarily have ADHD, but because knowledge about ADHD can be useful for understanding preschool hyperactivity. One essential component of this psychoeducation is to help parents understand that severe levels of hyperactivity are likely a result of biological factors rather than parenting. It is also important to emphasize that hyperactive preschoolers are not intentionally being disruptive. This can help parents understand the importance of channeling children's hyperactivity rather than attempting to eliminate it. Although it will not be explicitly presented to parents in the program, it is important for group leaders to be aware that a high percentage of children with ADHD also experience oppositional defiant disorder (ODD), and they should be prepared to answer questions parents may have about this disorder.

Developmental Issues

This session ends by discussing the importance of considering developmental issues. Parents in the group are likely to have children at various developmental stages, and it is important to keep in mind that strategies will likely need to be adapted depending on where the child is in development. For example, language will need to be simpler for children with less developed language skills.

Session 1 Curriculum

Materials Needed

- Whiteboard or poster
- Behavior Problems and Normal Development handout
- Managing Hyperactive Behavior worksheet
- Parenting Beliefs and Values worksheet
- What Helps You Parent Effectively? worksheet

Outline

- Introduce group leaders and members
- Establish group rules
- Introduce the program approach
- Give an overview of today's session
- Introduce hyperactivity in preschoolers and define ADHD
- Discuss managing hyperactive behavior
- Discuss developmental considerations
- Assign homework

Introductions

Begin the first session by welcoming members to the group. Introduce yourselves as group leaders.

Next have group members briefly introduce themselves, including the following information about their children:

- Name and age of children

- Main concerns

- Child strengths

Group Rules

Explain why it is important to establish group rules. Here is a suggested script:

Before we begin, we would like to establish some ground rules. This group involves learning about specific strategies from us, but it also provides an opportunity for you to share your individual experiences with your children and with different parenting strategies. Our group can brainstorm about how to adjust strategies to work best for your individual child. So it is important that everyone feels comfortable talking and listening in the group.

Write all the group rules on a whiteboard or poster. Explain rules and ask if anyone has additions. Standard group rules include the following:

- Confidentiality and its limits (this applies to both group leaders and members)

- One person talks at a time

- Step up, step back

  - Suggested script: *If you tend to be someone who talks a lot during discussions, try to let others have a turn, and if you tend to be someone who does not talk a lot, we would love to hear from you.*

- Be respectful, even if you disagree with someone's opinion (*this includes disagreements between partners*)

Program Approach

Explain that this program takes a collaborative approach, and make the following points.

A Collaborative Approach

Use the following script to emphasize the collaborative nature of this program:

We will be presenting specific strategies, talking about how to make the strategies work for your individual child, and giving you an opportunity to practice the strategies both during sessions and at home. Although we have suggestions about what sorts of approaches and techniques are generally helpful for hyperactive preschoolers, you are the expert on your child, so we will be putting our knowledge together to come up with ideas about how to apply these principles and techniques in your family. Every child reacts differently to strategies, and one of the advantages of coming to a group like this, as opposed to simply reading a parenting book, is that we can put all of our minds together to figure out how to tailor strategies to work best for your child."

Expectations

- Encourage parents to have positive but realistic expectations by reviewing the following. Parents may have tried some of these approaches without success. Point out that some children respond well to one type of strategy, whereas other children respond better to other types of strategies. However, sometimes small changes in how parents use a strategy can make a world of difference. Also, some strategies only work when other strategies are in place. So ask parents to try these approaches with an open mind, even if they have tried them before without success.

- Parents may already be using some of these strategies successfully. Encourage them to share their success stories with others in the group.

- Explain to parents that these techniques will only help if they continue to use them, using this suggested script:

  - *Eyeglasses do not fix your vision; they simply help you to see as long as you are wearing them. One of the other benefits of being in a group like this is that it can help parents stick with strategies that are sometimes hard to keep up.*

- Point out that change is likely to be gradual, with ups and downs, and that parents should try not to get discouraged during the down times.

- Emphasize the importance of attending every meeting, because each week the program will build on concepts from the previous week. Let parents know that if they need to miss a meeting for some reason, they should let a group leader know so that a time can be arranged to meet individually to catch up.

Overview of Today's Session

Explain that today the group will lay a foundation for the rest of the sessions. The group will discuss a number of general issues that are important to understand before learning specific strategies. Then, beginning next week, the group will explore specific strategies each week (point to the session titles on a handout).

Hyperactivity in Preschoolers

Introduce hyperactivity in preschoolers. Here is a suggested script:

This program is designed for families with hyperactive preschoolers. Although most preschoolers are very active, preschoolers who are even more active and impulsive than other children of the same age often have difficulties. Some of your children may outgrow their hyperactivity and their behavior may be just a phase. But some of your children may be showing behavior because they have ADHD. We would like to give you some information about ADHD, because even if your child does not have ADHD, understanding more about the disorder and symptoms may be helpful for you in understanding your child's hyperactivity.

What is ADHD?

Ask parents what they already know about the disorder. Provide the group with the Behavior Problems and Normal Development handout.

Here is a suggested script for introducing ADHD:

ADHD is a developmental delay in children's ability to regulate/control their own behavior. In other words, they have difficulty putting the brakes on their behavior. This leads to problems with hyperactivity, impulsivity (acting without thinking), and inattention, which are the main symptoms of ADHD.

Write the 3 core symptoms on the board and ask the group for examples. Provide the examples here to supplement their examples.

Hyperactivity

- Not being able to sit still
- Constantly on the go
- Being loud
- Being a chatterbox

Impulsivity

- Doing risky things (jumping from high places, running into the street)
- Interrupting/intruding on other peoples' activities

Inattention

- Difficulty focusing for long periods of time, particularly on activities that do not have immediate feedback
- Trouble listening/following directions

Emphasize that all children are hyperactive, impulsive, or inattentive sometimes, but with ADHD, these behaviors happen much more often than in other kids of the same age. Note that some children with ADHD only have trouble with attention and are not hyperactive or impulsive.

Explain that children with ADHD have trouble with one particular kind of attention. They have trouble working on a task when there is no immediate feedback or reward for what they are doing. Often, they can easily pay attention to television, videos, or computer games but have difficulty sitting at the dinner table. They often get drawn away from the task at hand by other, more interesting or fun things that are going on around them.

ADHD in Different Situations

Discuss how children with ADHD behave differently in different situations. Ask group members:

In what types of situations does your child tend to behave better or worse?

Use group members' ideas to generate the following categories:

- New situations vs. familiar situations

- One-on-one vs. group settings

- Interacting with mothers vs. fathers

- Structured vs. unstructured situations

- Interesting vs. boring tasks

- Preschool/daycare vs. home

Make the following points during the discussion:

- Just because children can pay attention in certain situations does not mean that parents should expect that they can pay attention in other situations.

- The fact that their behavior can be so variable makes it seem like they have some control over their behavior, and that they are purposely not listening to parents or other adults—that is not the case.

- The problem is not a matter of knowledge (knowing what they are supposed to do or not do)—it is a matter of being able to control their behavior.

ADHD as a Biological Disorder

Note that ADHD is primarily a biological disorder with a genetic basis. Highlight the following points:

- Because ADHD is genetic, it is quite common to see ADHD symptoms in multiple members of the family.

- Sometimes parents blame themselves or their children for ADHD symptoms, but in fact this disorder is not caused by poor parenting, and children with ADHD have little control over these symptoms.

- Just because ADHD is genetic does not mean that the behaviors associated with ADHD cannot be affected by a child's environment. In fact, children with ADHD are very sensitive to their environments, and parenting practices can make a big difference in how well a child with ADHD is able to function.

Developmental Changes in ADHD

Discuss how ADHD symptoms change during the preschool years, noting the following:

- Children with ADHD usually begin to show symptoms by the age of 3. Hyperactivity and impulsivity usually appear first, whereas inattention is sometimes not evident until children reach school age.

- In young preschoolers, hyperactivity and impulsivity will often involve larger physical movements, such as climbing on furniture, difficulty staying seated, and intruding on others. As children get older, they may show more subtle symptoms, such as being fidgety.

- As children get older and enter kindergarten, they are likely to begin to have more difficulties with being disorganized, forgetful, making careless mistakes in their work, and blurting out answers in class.

Managing Hyperactive Behavior

Begin a discussion on how to manage hyperactive behavior with the following points:

- Parents cannot make their children stop being hyperactive, but they can manage their children's hyperactive behavior so that it is less disruptive.

- Hyperactive children tend to be drawn to the most interesting and stimulating things in their environment. This may be the reason why they can typically pay attention to television for long periods of time—it is often the most interesting and stimulating thing in the environment! Many times the most interesting and stimulating thing in the environment involves something that is disruptive or unsafe (e.g., running away in public, climbing on furniture).

Channeling a Child's Hyperactivity

Make the following suggestions on how to channel a child's hyperactivity. Parents can:

- Create situations in which children can be active in ways that will not be disruptive or dangerous.

- Create a space in the home where children can be very active without hurting themselves or anyone/anything else.

- Set household rules that allow activity in safe ways and distinguish between hyperactive behavior that is not allowed and hyperactive behavior that is permitted. For example:

  - *No running in the kitchen, but running is allowed in the living room. It is okay to throw soft balls in the hallway, but not in the kitchen or living room.*

- Make the most interesting/stimulating thing in the environment something that is appropriate. For example:

  - Have a stash of "fidget activities" on hand, especially for situations that parents expect will be difficult for a child.

  - Make a list of appropriate activities that the child enjoys (use pictures of these activities for children who are not yet readers). Put it on the refrigerator, or somewhere else where it can be easily seen. If a child's high activity is causing disruption, parents can point to the list and redirect the child toward one of these activities.

Note that many children who are hyperactive also have difficulties with sensory regulation. They may be very sensitive to sounds, sights, or touch, or they may seek stimulation. If parents suspect this may be the case for their children, they may want to see an occupational therapist for help with these issues.

Discussion: Managing Hyperactive Behavior

To open up the discussion, ask group members:

- *What kinds of hyperactive behaviors would be okay for your child in your house?*

- *What kinds of hyperactive behaviors are not allowed?*

Have group members complete the Managing Hyperactive Behavior worksheet.

Developmental Considerations

Continue the session with a review of developmental considerations, covering the following topics.

Stages of Development

Note that earlier the group discussed how individual children respond differently to different strategies, but it is also true that children respond differently to strategies depending on their stage of development. For example, something that did not work when a child was 3 years old may work beautifully when she is 5.

Explain that children change rapidly between the ages of 2 and 6. Children's verbal skills grow dramatically over this period, they are able to understand more complicated ideas, gain greater self-control, have a greater capacity for empathy, and become more and more interested in peers. Emphasize that one of the challenges of parenting preschoolers is how much parents have to constantly adapt how they parent their children and adjust their expectations.

Developmental Differences

Emphasize that it is also important to not only consider the age of a child but where she is developmentally. For example, children's verbal skills develop at very different rates, so it will be important for parents to think about a child's verbal skills and what she is capable of understanding. Tell parents that it is important that they do not assume that just because other children of the same age can do something, their child is necessarily ready to do it.

Transitions

Note that preschool children often face many transitions, both in their daily lives (e.g., going to and leaving preschool), as well as big life transitions (e.g., a birth or adoption of a sibling, beginning kindergarten, moving). At the same time, preschool children do not always have the cognitive and emotional skills needed to adjust to these transitions. It is common for children to act out when they are overwhelmed by changes, and this may be particularly true of hyperactive preschoolers. Providing children with additional support and helping them anticipate and cope with transitions may prevent difficult behavior.

Homework

Explain that the next session will begin with a general discussion of parenting, so group members will need to think more about their own parenting this next week in preparation for the discussion.

✎ Have parents complete the Parenting Beliefs and Values worksheet. Explain to parents that they will not have to share their responses with the group unless they wish to do so.

✎ Have parents complete the What Helps You Parent Effectively? worksheet.

CHAPTER 4

Session 2: Using Praise Effectively

Session 2 Notes to Group Leaders

Overview

This session builds on session 1 by continuing to discuss general issues that lay an important foundation for learning specific parenting strategies. In particular, the group will have an opportunity to discuss some general parenting issues and review learning principles on which many of the strategies in this program are based, before focusing on the parenting tool presented in this session: praise.

Discussion of Parenting

This session begins by providing an opportunity to have some general discussions about parenting. Many of the tools that are presented can be challenging to implement; therefore, it is important to let parents know that one need not be a perfect parent to be an effective parent. Introducing this concept helps to prevent parents from being overly critical of themselves, which may interfere with their ability to be a good parent. It also sets the stage for parents to feel comfortable sharing any difficulties in using the strategies taught in this program.

The discussion of parenting also includes an acknowledgment that parenting is a balancing act, and that they will often be asked to engage in two different practices that may sometimes appear to be contradictory but, in fact, are complementary. For example, parents will be encouraged to be both warm (using praise and positive attention) and firm (setting limits and giving consequences). Although some parents are naturally able to combine these two types of practices (authoritative parenting; Baumrind, 1971), other parents emphasize one type of practice over the other.

Concepts of Reinforcement and Punishment

A number of the strategies included in this program are based on important learning principles, and it can be useful to begin by helping parents understand these principles. This session introduces the concepts of *reinforcement* and *punishment.* The most important concept to convey to parents during this discussion is that when something pleasant follows a behavior, the behavior is more likely to occur again in the future (reinforcement), and when something unpleasant follows a behavior, the behavior is less likely to occur again in the future (punishment). It can also be useful to introduce the notion that both children's and parents' behavior is shaped by its consequences. Although the basic concepts of reinforcement and punishment are not difficult, the notion that behavior can be reinforced or punished either by having something pleasant or unpleasant happen (positive reinforcement or positive punishment) or by having something pleasant or unpleasant taken away (negative reinforcement or negative punishment) can sometimes be confusing for parents. It is best to avoid the use of technical terms (e.g., negative reinforcement) in this discussion. Instead, a discussion that focuses on multiple examples is most useful. Examples are provided in the curriculum that group leaders can present, but we also recommend having the group generate examples from their own experiences.

Praise

The first tool presented in this program is praise. The program begins with praise because hyperactive children tend to receive more than their fair share of criticism (Danforth et al., 1991). When children receive so much negative attention for their behavior, a vicious cycle can occur in which parents and children are increasingly negative with each other (Patterson, 2002). Thus, praise can be an effective tool to encourage (reinforce) appropriate behavior and help break negative cycles that may have developed in the parent–child relationship. Praise is also thought to be to be an important part of creating a warm and nurturing parent–child relationship, which has clearly been shown to foster children's development (Kochanska, Forman, Aksan, & Dunbar, 2005).

Finally, there is some evidence that children who are hyperactive may be particularly responsive to praise (Kohls, Herpertz-Dahlmann, & Konrad, 2009).

Parents are likely to have received mixed messages and have conflicting feelings about the use of praise. Praise has received a great deal of media attention in recent years, and some have questioned the use of too much praise (Weissbourd, 2009). Any concerns that parents may have about the use of praise should be addressed upfront. It should be emphasized that *how* one praises is as important as *whether* one praises. Praise is most effective when it is genuine and specific (Henderlong & Lepper, 2002).

Although both theory and research provide support for the use of genuine and specific praise, parents should be aware that it is not a magic cure. While praise has been shown to be effective, the short-term effects on behavior have been fairly modest and smaller than the effects of many of the other tools taught in this program (Owen, Slep, & Heyman, 2012). However, there is a great deal of research suggesting that warm and nurturing parenting—what some have called a "mutually responsive orientation"—has long-term benefits for children (Kochanska et al., 2005). So even if the short-term effects of praise on children's misbehavior are modest, parents should be encouraged to continue praising their children's appropriate behavior with the expectation that the longer term benefits are likely to be even greater.

Session 2 Curriculum

Materials Needed

- Being a Balanced Parent handout

- Learning Principles handout

- Praise handout

- Catching Your Child Being Good worksheet

- Catching Your Child Being Good Log

Outline

- Review homework

- Discuss general issues in parenting

- Review homework, sharing parenting values and beliefs

- Introduce learning principles, including punishment and reinforcement

- Introduce praise and its importance

- Discuss how to praise and conduct in-session exercises

- Assign homework

Homework Review

Review homework from last session (approximately 10 to 15 minutes). Encourage parents to discuss their thoughts on what it was like to complete the Parenting Beliefs and Values worksheet. Be clear that parents do not have to share their responses to the questions on this assignment unless they would like to do so. Often parents have not explicitly thought about their beliefs about parenting, and they have many reactions to thinking about these issues. This is a good opportunity to discuss shared values as well as individual differences in parenting values and beliefs. Emphasize the importance of respecting others' values while being open to taking a closer look at one's own values and considering whether they are consistent with parents' goals for their children.

General Issues in Parenting

Before introducing specific parenting strategies, spend some time discussing parenting more generally with the group. Highlight the following points:

- Parenting is a very challenging job (particularly parenting hyperactive preschoolers) that no one really prepares parents for—children do not come with instructions.

- There are two big challenges in parenting: (1) figuring out what to do, and (2) doing it. This program addresses both, but acknowledges that many of the strategies are much easier said than done.

- There is no such thing as a "perfect" parent; parents should not expect that of themselves. Instead, they should simply try their best. If children needed perfect parents, we would all be in a lot of trouble.

- Parents should be encouraged to cultivate compassion for themselves. Acknowledge that this is an incredibly hard job! Feeling guilty about what they could have done "better" ultimately gets in the way of their ability to parent and to be present for their children.

- It can be helpful for parents to maintain a sense of humor.

- It can also be helpful for parents to share their frustrations and questions with friends who are parenting preschoolers as well. This is one of the reasons that this program takes place in a group setting.

Striking a Balance

Note that parenting hyperactive preschoolers often involves striking a balance between apparent opposites. Refer to the Being a Balanced Parent handout. Ask parents where they think they tend to lean on each of the following dimensions.

- Warmth -------- firmness

- Flexibility -------- control

- Accepting your child -------- trying to change your child

- Meeting your child's needs -------- meeting your own needs

For the last dimension, emphasize to group members that their children are very important, but taking care of themselves so that they can be the best parents they can be is also very important.

As part of the program, the group will be talking about how to strike a balance between both ends of these demensions, which often means embracing two seemingly opposite goals.

Beliefs about Parenting

Note that people learn how to parent by watching other parents (especially their own parents) in their community, by trial and error, and by reading about parenting and child rearing. Because individuals have different personal and cultural experiences, parents in the group will likely all have somewhat different beliefs about parenting and what "good" parenting looks like. Describe the role of beliefs in this program as a segue to the homework review. Here is a sample script:

Your beliefs about parenting—your values and goals—are very important. We asked you to think about these over this past week, because it is important to think about how what we are suggesting over the course of this program fits in with your own beliefs and values about child rearing.

Understanding Learning Principles

Explain to the group that before the leaders start discussing specific techniques, it is important to understand some basic ideas about how behavior can be shaped by its consequences. The following script may be used:

There are some important learning principles that shape both parent and child behavior. Many of the strategies we will discuss are based on these ideas, so we want to give you a brief introduction to these principles. As we go through the program we will come back to these again.

Provide group members with the Learning Principles handout to review.

Reinforcement

Define reinforcement as increasing behavior with consequences.

- If something *pleasant happens* after a child does something, the child is *more likely* to do it again in the future. For example:

  - *If a child is given dessert when he says, "Please, may I have dessert," he will be more likely to say "please" in the future.*

  - *A child cooperates at bedtime and is rewarded with an extra story. The child will be more likely to cooperate at bedtime in the future.*

- If something *unpleasant stops* after a child does something, the child is *more likely* to do it again in the future. For example:

  - *A mother asks her child to pick up his toys. The child starts screaming, and the mother says, "Forget it, I'll do it myself!" The child has learned that screaming makes an unpleasant thing (a mother asking him to pick up his toys) stop, and will be more likely to scream in this situation in the future.*

Punishment

Define punishment as decreasing behavior with consequences:

- If something *unpleasant happens* after a child does something, the child is *less likely* to do it in the future. For example:

  - *A child takes a toy from another child and the other child hits him. The child learns not to grab toys (although he also may be learning to hit).*

- If something *pleasant is taken away* after a child does something, the child is *less likely* to do it in the future. For example:

  - *A child draws on the wall with markers, so his father takes away the markers. The child will be less likely to draw on the wall next time.*

Beyond Reinforcement and Punishment

Explain that these principles are not the only things that shape children's behavior—they are just one important set of factors. There are some parenting practices that may reinforce or punish behavior the way parents might like but may have other negative effects on children, especially in the long run. For example, screaming or calling a child names might be punishing, and might stop a child from engaging in a behavior in the short term, but it can also affect the child's emotional well-being, which in turn can have negative effects on behavior in the long term.

Learning Principles and Parents' Behavior

Note that parents' behavior can also be shaped by consequences.

- Parenting practices can be reinforced by children's behavior. For example:

  - *A parent yells at her child and the child listens. The parent's yelling has been reinforced by something good happening (child listening).*

  - *A child whines and complains when his father says he cannot have a cookie. The father says, "Oh fine!" and gives the child a cookie and the whining stops. The father's giving in is reinforced when the child's whining stops.*

- Parenting practices can be punished by children's behavior. For example:

- *A mother tells her child that he cannot have a cookie and her child starts screaming. The mother's setting a firm limit may be punished by the child's screaming.*

- *A child is sitting quietly at the dinner table and a parent says, "I like how nicely you are sitting." The child gets very excited by the compliment and hops out of his seat. The parent's use of praise may be punished by the child not staying seated at the dinner table.*

Accidental Consequences

Explain that sometimes parents can accidentally reward or punish behavior in ways that are counterproductive. Use the following questions for discussion:

- *What are some ways that you accidentally reward your child's negative behavior?*

- *What are some ways that your child accidentally rewards your negative parenting behavior?*

Importance of Consistency and Picking Battles

Explain that the consequence does not have to happen every time for it to affect behavior. If children never get what they want when they whine, they are likely to stop whining. However, if children find that they get their way about half the time when they whine, most children will take those odds and whine. Here is a suggested script for conveying to the group how to be more consistent:

Because it can be very difficult to be consistent, it is critical that you "pick your battles." If you are going to ask your child to do something, you need to follow through with a consequence if they do not, every time. Do not threaten anything you cannot follow through on (e.g., leaving your kid in the store if they do not stop screaming). If you cannot follow through, do not make the request. Through this program you will learn tools to set effective limits and consistently enforce them.

That said, no parent is perfect and it is not possible to be consistent 100% of the time. Your goal is to be as consistent as you possibly can, but it is also important not to be hard on yourself if you notice that you are not being consistent. When you notice yourself being inconsistent, think about why you were not able to be consistent and think about whether there was something you could have done to be more consistent. If you find that there is a situation where you cannot enforce a rule, be clear with your child that this is a rare exception (and make sure it is!).

Introduction to Praise

Introduce praise using the following suggested script:

Hyperactive preschoolers often have difficulty following directions and rules, and their impulsive behavior can cause problems in their relationships with other children and adults. Although these children also often have a number of strengths, including being very enthusiastic, creative, and bright, it is easy to focus on what they are doing wrong rather than on what they are doing right. Therefore, they tend to get much more negative feedback than positive feedback. This negative feedback can lead to a vicious cycle. Hyperactive preschoolers often hear a great deal of criticism, which can lead them to view themselves negatively (note that their low self-esteem may not always be obvious—they sometimes seem to be overconfident), which in turn may lead to more difficult behavior and emotional problems down the road.

For the following sections, refer parents to the Praise handout.

Important Reasons to Praise

Review the following:

- Praising good behavior makes it more likely that the good behavior will happen again.

- Praising children is likely to help them see themselves positively, which in turn leads to emotional well-being and good behavior.

- Praise is thought to be to be an important part of creating a warm and nurturing parent–child relationship, which is important for children's development.

For a brief group discussion, have parents talk about a time when someone expressed appreciation for something they did well and the impact it had on them.

Reasons Why Parents Are Sometimes Hesitant to Praise

To foster discussion, ask group members the following questions:

- *How often do you praise?*

- *Are there times when you are hesitant to praise? If so, why?*

Following are reasons why parents are sometimes hesitant to praise. Discuss these reasons and review the suggested responses to these concerns.

Belief that Children Should not be Praised for Something that is a Basic Expectation

- Praise will help children to consistently meet basic expectations.

- Praising children for doing something does not imply that it is not a basic expectation. For example:

  - *As a parent, one of your basic expectations is to fix meals for your child. If your child tells you how delicious your cooking is, it would probably make you more motivated to cook good food for your child.*

- For a hyperactive child, things that seem like they should be basic expectations are often, in fact, quite difficult. Encourage parents to acknowledge this difficulty by praising their children for behaviors that do not come easily to them (even if they might come easily to other children).

Concern that Praising Children Will Make Them Spoiled or Full of Themselves

- Children get spoiled when parents do not set limits and when children get too many privileges, not from being praised too much.

- Hyperactive preschoolers are at risk for having low self-esteem, so there is really very little danger of them having an inflated sense of self-esteem in the long run. If a child seems to have an inflated sense of self-esteem now, that is normal at this age. Children will have plenty of opportunity to face the reality of their limitations. Emphasizing a child's limitations at home does not serve to protect him from this reality—quite the contrary.

- As children develop it is important to help them strike the balance between pride/self-esteem and modesty/not bragging. But this is typically a task that is best to focus on when children are older.

- In fact there is evidence that praise, when done effectively, increases internal motivation.

Children's Reaction to Praise

Review typical children's reactions to praise:

- Most children will be visibly pleased by praise.

- Hyperactive children may get excited and happy and become temporarily more hyperactive—encourage parents to not let this stop them from praising!

- Occasionally children, especially as they get older, may seem as though they do not want parents to praise them—they may roll their eyes or disagree with their parents. Again, encourage parents to not let this stop them!

How Should Parents Praise?

Note that there are many different ways to praise—parents will need to find a style that feels comfortable for them.

For discussion, tell parents to make a list of examples (10 to 20) of ways that they can praise their children that feel comfortable for them. Collect these and create a list of "Ways of Praising Your Child" that you can give to the group members next week.

Important Qualities of Praise

Review the following qualities of praise, giving examples.

- Be specific. For example:

  - *"I love how you came right away when I called you!"*

  - *"You are doing a great job of staying at the dinner table!"*

- Be genuine.

- Praise the behavior, not the child. Research suggests that praising the behavior will make children more resilient to future criticism. For example:

  - *"Nice job cleaning up your toys!" instead of, "Good boy!"*

  - *"I like your drawing," instead of, "You are a good drawer."*

- Praise effort. For example:

  - *"Wow, you are really working hard at that!"*

- Avoid praise that is mixed with criticism. For example:

  - *"Thank you for finally listening to me!"*

  - *"You did a great job staying near me in the grocery store. Why can't you do that every time?"*

In-Session Exercise: Role-Play

Engage in a role-play exercise in which parents can practice praising. Note that this is the first role-play, so it may be helpful to introduce it as follows:

Sometimes in this program we will be doing role-plays. We know that role-plays can be awkward and can feel different from real interactions with your child, but practicing them here can make it easier to bring the skills home, and it is also a good way for us to make sure that we are communicating well about what we would like you to do to at home.

Have the two group leaders first model the role-play. Leaders can then either break parents up into pairs, or leaders can have volunteers role-play in front of the group (with one leader role-playing as the child) and have the group give them feedback. Adults who are portraying children should generally be compliant in these scenarios to provide more opportunities for praise. Acknowledge to parents that this may not reflect real life but that parents will work toward more realistic scenarios in later sessions. Parents can create their own scenarios, or group leaders can suggest situations. Here are some examples to use:

- Bring in a set of blocks and have parents role-play a parent getting the child to clean up.

- Have parents role-play a parent trying to get a child ready in the morning or ready for bed.

- Have parents role-play eating together at dinnertime.

When and How Often Should Parents Praise?

Emphasize that praise should be given *as often as possible.*

Encourage parents to give praise anytime they notice their children *not misbehaving.* In other words, "Catch them being good." Note that this can be very difficult because it is much easier to notice bad behavior than the absence of bad behavior. Reiterate that children do not have to be doing something special to be praised—they just have to *not be misbehaving.*

It can also be difficult for parents to give praise if the children are playing happily, parents are finally getting a quiet moment, and they are worried about interrupting and spoiling the moment. Emphasize that in the long run, parents will get many more quiet moments if they express their appreciation for them.

In-Session Exercise: Catching Children Being Good

Before parents leave, help them fill out the Catching Your Child Being Good worksheet. Help parents identify one or two child misbehaviors that they would like to focus on this week. Then assist them in identifying the behavior that they would like to see instead of the misbehavior and deciding what they will say to praise the desired behavior.

Homework

Explain that when trying to do something new it sometimes helps to keep a log to remind oneself to do it. Tell parents that they will not have to do this forever—just while they are trying to change their habits.

- Have parents complete the Catching Your Child Being Good Log to record their efforts to praise.

CHAPTER 5

Session 3: Increasing Positive Interactions and Using Attention to Shape Children's Behavior

Session 3 Notes to Group Leaders

Overview

Session 3 builds on the principles that were taught in session 2. The goal of session 3 is to help parents increase the amount and quality of positive attention children receive and to use parental attention to help encourage appropriate behavior and discourage undesirable behavior. As noted in session 2, children with hyperactivity tend to receive considerable negative attention (Barkley, 2006), and this can result in escalating negative behavior on the part of both parent and child. By increasing the positive attention children receive, parents can interrupt this cycle. Together with praise, positive attention can be important in fostering a warm and nurturing parent–child relationship. Furthermore, positive attention is key because many preschoolers and their parents can fall into interaction patterns in which children get far more attention for misbehavior than they do for appropriate behavior. Shifting these patterns so that parental attention reinforces desirable behavior can help foster cycles in which positive child behavior elicits positive parent behavior and vice versa.

Positive Attention

In this session, parents are taught a form of positive attention that may be quite different from their typical way of interacting with their children. In particular, parents are encouraged to engage in one-on-one time with their children—time in which the activity is child-directed rather than parent-directed. Facilitating this type of interaction has been an important component in a number of other parenting programs (Herschell, Calzada, Eyberg, & McNeil, 2002; Webster-Stratton et al., 2011), and programs that place a heavy emphasis on this approach have been shown to be highly effective (Eisenstadt, Eyberg, McNeil, Newcomb, & Funderburk, 1993). This approach may be particularly helpful for hyperactive children whose parents are typically more directive than parents of typically developing children (Danforth et al., 1991).

Finding the Right Balance

Some parents may report that they already give their children a great deal of positive attention. It is important to brainstorm with parents to help them find a healthy balance between giving their children attention and meeting their own needs. During the session, group leaders should assess the degree to which parents need to increase positive attention. For parents who spend a great deal of time already interacting with their children, the goal may not be to increase the amount of time they spend with their children but instead to change the way they interact with their children during that time (e.g., using narration).

Barriers to Giving Positive Attention

The strategies taught in this session can be difficult for parents to carry out. Challenging, hyperactive behavior can sap parents' energy and elicit negative emotions from parents, making it difficult to initiate positive interactions with their children and ignore inappropriate attention-seeking behavior. It is important to acknowledge this and to brainstorm with parents about how they might be able to find the time and emotional energy to implement these strategies and have more positive interactions with their children.

Session 3 Curriculum

Materials Needed

- Positive Attention handout

- Using Attention and Ignoring to Shape Your Child's Behavior handout

- Positive Attention Log

- Playing Games with Preschool Children handout

Outline

- Review homework

- Introduce positive attention and conduct in-session exercise

- Discuss rewarding a child's appropriate behavior with positive attention and ignoring a child's attention-seeking negative behavior, and practice ignoring

- Assign homework

Homework Review

Begin by reviewing homework from the last session (approximately 10 minutes). Have group members share their Catching Your Child Being Good logs and briefly discuss successes and difficulties.

Introduction to Positive Attention

Introduce positive attention using the following suggested script:

Because hyperactive preschoolers can be difficult to manage, they often receive much more negative attention than positive attention. Although most children prefer positive attention to negative attention, they prefer some attention to no attention at all. In fact, preschoolers often enjoy getting a reaction from adults, even if it is a negative reaction. So although yelling may seem like something children would try to avoid, children may actually engage in behavior designed to get their parents to have a fit. Increasing the amount of positive attention children receive will decrease their attempts to seek out negative attention. Like praise, positive attention is also an important part of creating a warm and nurturing parent–child relationship. Positive attention can also be used to reward children's good behavior, and selective ignoring can be used to discourage certain types of negative behavior.

Note that it is healthy and adaptive for children to do things to get your attention. Rather than dismissing a child's attention-seeking behavior ("She's just doing that to get attention"), recognize it as an effort to communicate with you that she needs more attention. Giving children lots of attention will not spoil them.

Discussion: Positive Attention

To open up discussion, ask:

What are some ways that you give your child positive attention?

Ways of Giving Positive Attention

Review the following suggestions for giving children more positive attention. Refer parents to the Positive Attention handout.

Describing Children's Activities

- Encourage parents to use narration. They can pretend to be a narrator in a play—it is amazing how powerful it can be to simply describe children's behavior as they engage in activity. Here are some examples of what parents can say:

  - *"I see that you are lining up all of the trucks getting ready to put them in the garage."*

  - *"Oh my goodness, that race was really close!"*

  - *"You are drawing a huge castle. Look at those towers!"*

One-on-One Time

- Parents should try to find at least 10 minutes each day to focus on playing with their children.

- It can be helpful to find a specific time each day—for example, right before getting ready for bed.

- Parents should try to give undivided attention to the child in these interactions. Parents should try not to do other things (e.g., read, fold laundry) during their one-on-one time.

- Parents do not have to be playing interactively with the child during one-on-one time. It could be 10 minutes of parents actively watching, commenting, and describing the child's play.

- Parents can follow the child's interests, but should steer the child toward an activity that will be unlikely to lead to frustration or a great deal of limit setting.

- If the child misbehaves during one-on-one time, parents should simply stop the activity.

- If the child is being hyperactive during this time, parents should try not to discourage the hyperactivity unless it is dangerous or disruptive.

- If parents have multiple children, it may be very difficult to find time for one-on-one interactions. Parents can also give the child positive attention when they are caring for more than one child, so if they have difficulty finding time for one-on-one interactions with the child, they can focus their efforts on increasing the positive attention they give to all of their children.

- Although this takes extra effort initially, in the long run it should make life easier for parents because they will face less misbehavior.

Nonverbal Ways of Positively Attending

Review the following and brainstorm with the group additional ways of attending nonverbally.

- Eye contact (not just watching using peripheral vision)

- Warm/enthusiastic tone of voice

- Being physically close

- Physical affection

Discussion: One-on-One Time

To open up discussion, ask:

What are some things that may make it hard to have one-on-one time with your child?

Help troubleshoot problems that group members anticipate in implementing one-on-one time.

In-Session Exercise: Positive Attending

Have group leaders model positive attending skills using toys. Then give toys to parents, and have them practice positive attending skills. Encourage parents to use a mixture of positive attending techniques including narrating, nonverbal methods (just watching), and praise. Asking the child questions is fine, but encourage parents not to overdo it.

Rewarding Appropriate Behavior and Ignoring Negative Behavior

Explain that in addition to generally increasing the amount of positive attention a child gets, attention can be used to reward good behavior and ignore negative attention-seeking behavior. Refer parents to the Using Attention and Ignoring to Shape Your Child's Behavior handout.

Rewarding Appropriate Behavior with Positive Attention

Encourage parents to give their children positive attention when they are behaving well. For example:

If your child has been playing nicely for several minutes, you could say, "Look at that big castle you are making. I wonder if all of your knights will fit in it."

Deciding When to Ignore Behavior

Tell parents that in order to decide when they should ignore, they need to determine why their children are misbehaving. To open up discussion, ask:

What are some reasons why children misbehave?

Make a chart with "behavior" in one column and "reason" in a second column. Help parents generate a list of misbehaviors and discuss possible reasons for that behavior.

Common Reasons Why Children Misbehave

- To get something they want (e.g., treats, toys).

- To get out of doing something they do not want to do (e.g., going to bed).

- To get attention/a reaction.

- Because the misbehavior is fun or interesting.

  - Hyperactive children are particularly prone to this, because they tend to have difficulty stopping themselves from doing things that are fun in the short term but that have negative long-term consequences (e.g., putting cereal in the DVD player, drawing on the wall, jumping on the couch, throwing a ball in the kitchen).

■ There are, of course, things that make them more likely to misbehave, such as being hungry, tired, or upset.

Knowing the Reasons for the Misbehavior Can Help Parents Decide What to Do

Review the following guidelines for deciding when to ignore.

■ If the child is misbehaving to get attention or a reaction, removing all attention (ignoring) is typically the most effective strategy. If a parent yells at a child, it may make the child more likely to misbehave if she is misbehaving to get a reaction out of her parent. For example:

■ *Your child swears, looks for your reaction, and starts to giggle. She is probably doing this to get your attention.*

■ If a child is misbehaving because the misbehavior is fun, ignoring will not work. For example:

■ *Your child is jumping on the couch, but does not seem to be noticing you—she is probably jumping on the couch simply because it is fun and she does not have the behavioral control to stop herself. Ignoring will not likely work in this situation.*

■ Sometimes it can be hard to tell whether a child is misbehaving to get attention or for another reason. Thus, there is some trial and error in figuring out what to do.

■ It is common for the misbehavior to initially serve one purpose but, over time, to take on another purpose. For example, a child may initially be jumping on the couch because it is fun, but over time she realizes that it is a good way of getting attention.

■ A child may be doing something just to get attention, but if it is dangerous, parents should not ignore it. In this case, it is important to handle the misbehavior in a way that is as matter-of-fact and businesslike as possible, so that the child receives minimal attention.

How to Ignore

Review the following guidelines for effectively ignoring a child's misbehavior.

- Parents should not look at the child or talk to the child or talk about the child. They should walk away if it is safe to do so.

- If parents decide to ignore, they need to stick to it. Otherwise the child may figure out that she needs to misbehave for a long period of time before she gets what she wants.

- Parents need to be consistent about ignoring. If parents pay attention to the misbehavior one out of every four times, the child will figure out that she needs to engage in the misbehavior four times before she will get their attention.

- Ignoring will be far more effective if a child is receiving positive attention for good behavior. Parents should be on the lookout for good behavior and really give their children a great deal of positive attention when they are not engaging in misbehavior. Parents should resume ignoring if the misbehavior starts again.

Not Reacting as a Form of Ignoring

- Often it is not possible to completely ignore a child when she is misbehaving. The key is to interact with the child without reacting to the attention-seeking behavior. In other words, one can ignore the behavior without ignoring the child. For example:

  - *Your child hits you and laughs. If you yell at your child and give your child a lecture about not hitting, your child is likely to realize that she can get an interesting reaction out of you by hitting. Calmly giving your child a consequence, with as few words and facial expressions as you can manage, will teach your child that hitting leads to an unpleasant consequence rather than to an interesting reaction.*

Children's Reactions

Review children's typical reactions to having their misbehavior ignored.

- It is not uncommon for children to temporarily increase the misbehavior when parents ignore it, which can make it harder to ignore! It simply takes a few minutes for a child to realize that her parents are not going to pay attention to the behavior. The behavior should decrease after the initial increase, so parents should be patient. If it does not decrease, it is probably either because the child is still getting some attention (perhaps from someone else) or the behavior was not attention-seeking behavior.

■ If a child is engaging in a great deal of attention-seeking behavior, this may be a sign that she needs more positive attention, and parents may need to increase their efforts to give her positive attention.

Discussion: Children's Attention-Seeking Behavior

To open up discussion, ask:

■ *What are some positive and negative ways your child tries to get your attention?*

■ *Can the negative ways be ignored?*

In-Session Exercise: Ignoring

Role-play some of the situations that parents brainstormed during discussion, and practice ignoring negative attention-seeking behavior.

Homework

✎ Have parents spend 10 minutes per day engaging in one-on-one time with their children, using positive attending. They can keep track of their one-on-one time on the Positive Attention Log.

✎ Have parents read the Playing Games with Preschool Children handout (optional). Introduce this handout by letting parents know that challenges can sometimes arise when playing games with preschool children. This handout addresses those challenges.

CHAPTER 6

Session 4: Setting Up an Effective Reward System

Session 4 Notes to Group Leaders

Overview

This session continues to highlight positive approaches to encouraging appropriate behavior in children. Tangible rewards or incentives can be helpful in encouraging children to accomplish tasks that are particularly challenging for them or to learn new behaviors (Cameron, Banko, & Pierce, 2001). This session focuses on both unplanned rewards, which parents can give spontaneously for desirable behavior, and planned rewards, in the form of reward systems.

Reward Systems

It can be very challenging for parents to develop an effective reward system. Therefore, most of the session is devoted to helping parents create a reward system, which will consist of a "contract" that outlines what rewards the child will earn for which behaviors. As group leaders are helping parents develop their systems, it is important to remember that children should not be given tangible rewards for behaviors they already do easily or for engaging in activities that they already find intrinsically rewarding, since tangible rewards can decrease the child's internal motivation in such situations (Cameron et al., 2001). Instead, reward systems should be used for establishing new patterns of behavior or breaking out of negative cycles. As group leaders help parents design reward systems, it is essential to create a reward program that is realistic for parents to carry out. Even the most perfectly designed reward program will not be effective if parents cannot consistently implement it at home.

Common Concerns About Using Rewards

Parents (and sometimes group leaders) may have strong reactions to the notion of using tangible rewards. A common concern voiced by parents is that tangible rewards are "bribery." Group leaders will need to address these concerns early in the session. Leaders may find it helpful to emphasize that bribes are used to get someone to do something immoral or illegal. In contrast, tangible rewards will be used to encourage *appropriate* behavior. Additionally, parents may say that they have tried using rewards in the past unsuccessfully. This is often because of common mistakes. This session will help parents avoid such mistakes, thus increasing the likelihood that the reward system will be successful.

Session 4 Curriculum

Materials Needed

- Setting Up a Reward Program handout

- Sample Reward System handout

- Child's Sticker Path worksheet

- Other Types of Reward Charts handout

Outline

- Review homework from last session

- Introduce the use of incentives/rewards

- Discuss reasons why parents are sometimes reluctant to use incentives

- Present steps for setting up a reward program

- Complete in-session exercises to have parents select behaviors, decide on rewards, and create a chart

- Give guidance on how to implement the reward program at home

- Assign homework

Homework Review

Review parents' Positive Attention Logs (approximately 10 minutes). Discuss any challenges parents faced in spending one-on-one time or using positive attending with children.

Introduction to Rewards

Introduce rewards using the following suggested script:

There are so many changes during the preschool years—children are learning how to do more and more things for themselves (e.g., getting dressed, putting toys away), but they are not yet able to do these things for themselves 100% of the time. This can be a challenging time for all preschoolers and their parents, but especially for parents of hyperactive preschoolers.

One way to help children learn these new behaviors and expectations is to use rewards to motivate children as they learn new behaviors. Rewards should not be used for everything. They should be used less than praise and should be saved for encouraging children to accomplish tasks that are particularly difficult for them—things like getting dressed on time in the morning, getting ready for bed, playing cooperatively with a sibling, or picking up toys. Even when you use rewards, you should combine them with praise. Rewards can be used spontaneously to encourage positive behavior, or reward systems can be put in place in which children are told ahead of time how behaviors will be rewarded.

Issues to Consider in Using Reward Systems

Discuss with the group the following issues regarding reward systems:

- Reward systems often work very well at the beginning and lose their effectiveness over time as the novelty wears off and as parents forget to implement them consistently.

- Reward systems are especially good for establishing new habits or patterns of behavior and breaking out of negative cycles.

- It is important that all adults in the house are consistent in using the system. If there is more than one adult in a household taking care of the child, parents should make sure that everyone agrees on the system before beginning.

- Sometimes younger preschoolers are not quite ready for these types of reward systems. If a child does not seem to understand the system, first try to simplify the system. If that does not work, wait a few months and try again.

Reasons Why Parents are Sometimes Reluctant to Use Incentives

Review the following concerns parents often have about using incentives. Suggested responses to these concerns are provided.

Concern That Giving Incentives to a Child Is a Form of Bribery

Bribery is when you give someone something to get them to do something immoral or illegal. You will be rewarding your child for appropriate behaviors that you are trying to encourage. Just like your paycheck is not a bribe, using incentives to encourage appropriate behavior is not a bribe.

Concern About Giving an Incentive for Something a Child Is Expected to Be Doing

The reason you are deciding to use incentives is because the behavior is challenging for your child, and he needs some extra help starting to do it. You are not going to reward it forever. Once it becomes habit, you will fade out your reward program. Again, adults get incentives and rewards even for things they are expected to do (e.g., getting a paycheck for going to work).

Concern That Giving a Child Incentives Will Decrease the Child's Internal Motivation for Behaving Well

There are some situations where giving rewards can decrease a child's internal motivation. This is usually when you give a reward for something that the child can already do and likes doing. However, we are not talking about giving rewards for those behaviors, but only for those behaviors that seem to be challenging for your child. In other words, you are using rewards to get the ball rolling. Getting a bonus for doing good work at your job does not decrease your motivation to do good work, right? It increases it.

Parents Who Have Already Tried Unsuccessfully to Give Rewards

Many parents say they have already tried reward programs, and that they have not worked. This is often because of common mistakes in setting up a reward program. Let's talk about the main principles of how to use rewards to address these common problems.

Setting Up a Reward Program

For preschoolers, sticker programs are a helpful form of reward system. (Provide parents with the examples in the accompanying handouts). In these programs, parents reward a child's behavior with a sticker (which goes on the chart; parents can also draw stars if they are out of stickers or think the child does not care about stickers). When a child has accumulated enough stickers, he can earn a prize or privilege.

Talk through the specifics of the reward system with the group, referring parents to the Setting Up a Reward Program handout and the Sample Reward Charts. Encourage parents to use the Child's Sticker Path worksheet as they learn the steps.

Choose General Behavior to Target

Review the following guidelines for choosing behavior to target with the reward program.

- Encourage parents to choose one or two behaviors at a time to avoid overwhelming the parent or the child. Trying to address too many behaviors at once can be a problem. A child may become overwhelmed, and parents will have difficulty monitoring the target behaviors and rewarding the child's behavior consistently. Instead, parents should consider the frequency with which each behavior occurs.

For example:

- If it is something that will require monitoring throughout the day, then it is probably realistic to only focus on that behavior.

- If it is something that occurs only once a day (e.g., getting ready for daycare/preschool in the morning), parents could also consider adding something that regularly occurs at another time of day.

- Remind parents to take into account the child's developmental stage and personality. They should be sure to choose something that the child is capable of doing, and keep in mind that hyperactive preschoolers may not be capable of doing some of the things that other preschoolers might be able to do (e.g., sitting quietly for 30 minutes at dinner).

- Behaviors associated with hyperactivity can be shaped by reward systems. One might assume that because hyperactivity is genetic, it cannot be changed. It is true that hyperactivity cannot be changed permanently, but, in fact, behaviors associated with hyperactivity can be affected by consequences. Hyperactive behaviors are typically caused by children having difficulty putting on the brakes, but reward systems can assist children in applying the brakes. Note that as soon as the reward system is stopped, the child's hyperactive behavior will return. The reward system is like eyeglasses that help people to see but only when they are wearing them.

- Parents should consider what is realistic for them—they should consider their family, schedule, and obligations. Close monitoring will be important for the success of the reward system they develop.

In-Session Exercise: Choosing Behavior

Encourage parents to complete the "What I am working on" section of the Sticker Path worksheet to indicate which behavior they will have their children focus on in the reward program.

Specifying What the Child Must Do to Earn Stickers

Give parents the following instructions for describing what their children need to do to earn stickers/stars.

- Whenever possible, parents should think about what behavior they would like to see, rather than focusing on what they do not want to see. For example:

  - *Instead of "Do not run away from mom at the store," your child's goal might be, "Stay close to mom at the store."*

  - *Instead of "No screaming," your child's goal might be, "Talk with an inside voice."*

- There are some cases in which it is very difficult to think of a positive way to frame the behavior. In those cases, it is fine to say what the negative behavior is, but it is helpful to specify a period of time. For example:

  - *Instead of "Do not beg for a cookie," your child's goal might be, "Go for an hour without begging for a cookie."*

- Parents should be specific about the behavior they want to see. This is critical for the program to work. It needs to be clear to parents *and* the child when a sticker has been earned. Many reward programs have problems when the behavior is not specific or clear enough. For example, it is not clear enough to say, "You will get a sticker if you are good during dinner." That is too vague, especially for a preschooler. Parents need to first determine what "being good" really means in terms of concrete behaviors. Examples of specific behaviors in this case might be:

  - *"Staying at the table until excused."*

  - *"Talking in a sweet voice—not whining, complaining, or screaming."*

- Parents should write the behavior down, even though their children cannot read (this will help remind parents).

- Parents can draw simple pictures next to the words to help their children remember what it says.

In-Session Exercise: Specifying What Children Need to Do to Earn Stickers

Encourage parents to complete the "How can I earn stickers/stars" section of the Sticker Path worksheet to indicate which specific behaviors their children will need to engage in to earn stickers.

Choosing Rewards

- Emphasize that rewards do *not* need to be big and expensive. Preschoolers are motivated by small prizes and extra privileges.

- Parents should keep rewards varied to maintain the child's interest.

- Children can get involved in the process by helping to identify rewards.

Brainstorm with the group about privileges and prizes that can be used as rewards.

- Examples of privileges

  - *An extra story at bedtime*

  - *Having a special dessert*

  - *A small amount of extra TV or computer time*

  - *Getting to stay up 10 minutes later than usual*

  - *A special outing*

  - *Doing a special activity with a parent*

- Recommend the use of a grab bag or prize box. For example:

  - *Putting small prizes (e.g., toys, craft supplies, temporary tattoos) in a special "grab bag" or "prize box" can make these items even more appealing to preschoolers. When the child has earned enough stickers, he would get to pick a prize out of the grab bag or prize box.*

Encourage parents to choose which rewards their children can earn.

Translating Stickers into Rewards

Next, have parents decide how many stickers each behavior earns and then how many stickers must be earned before a child earns a prize.

Advise parents on how to pace the steps correctly. They should try not to make it too difficult or too easy to earn stickers/stars and prizes. Note the following:

- This can take some trial and error.

- Programs often fail when the steps and expectations are so large that children become frustrated and give up.

- A reward program that works will involve small steps on the way to an ultimate goal.

- If parents are unsure how big to make the steps, they can observe the child for a day or two and see how often the target behavior is already occurring.

- Generally it is better to make it easier to earn a reward initially, make it a little more difficult as the child starts to master the behavior, and then phase out the reward once he has mastered the behavior.

In-Session Exercise: Translating Stickers into Rewards

Have parents decide how many stickers each behavior will earn and how many stickers need to be earned before their children can receive a reward. Have parents complete the "What can I get with my stickers?" section of the Sticker Path worksheet. (Let parents know that they can use different quantities of stickers than those indicated on the worksheet if appropriate.)

Implementing the Reward Program at Home

Introducing the Sticker Program to the Child

Recommend the following steps:

- Pick a time when both parent and child are (relatively) calm and have time to talk and listen.

- Introduce the program on a positive note. For example:

  - *You might say to your child, "There are lots of nice things you do. Sometimes you have trouble getting dressed on time in the morning and we all get frustrated. This sticker chart will help you learn how to get dressed in the morning without everybody getting frustrated and you get a chance to earn prizes!"*

- Show the chart to the child.

- Review each behavior on the chart and explain what is expected in order to receive a sticker.

- Explain that the chart will stay empty if he does not do the behavior.

- Involve the child by having him decorate the chart, select stickers for the chart, and decide where to place the chart.

- Go over the list of rewards with the child and get his input (within reason) about things he would like to earn as prizes.

- End the discussion on a positive note. For example:

    - *"I am glad we could talk about how to make getting dressed in the mornings easier!"*

- It may be helpful to model the behavior that will earn the child a sticker and model the behavior that will not earn the child a sticker, and then have him practice the behavior that will earn him a sticker.

  Remind parents that it is good to involve their children in setting up the program within reason, but parents are ultimately in charge of the program!

Things to Keep in Mind When Using a Reward System

Review with the group the following guidelines on effectively using a reward system. Below are suggested scripts.

- Remember, appropriate behavior, *then* reward:
  Your child must behave appropriately before he gets the sticker. If he gets a sticker before the behavior or when he has only "sort of" done the behavior, it will not work, because you will not actually be reinforcing the behavior that you want to encourage. You will be reinforcing some other (potentially problematic) behavior.

- Reward immediately:
  You should give your child the sticker as immediately following the behavior as possible. This is especially important for hyperactive preschoolers, who have a poorly developed sense of time and who are most strongly motivated by immediate rewards.

- Be aware that rewards will not last:
  Reward systems will stop working after a while—they are best for trying to help establish new habits. If your system is losing its effectiveness, changing it can often help it be effective again. Try new prizes or a new chart.

Homework

- Have parents make a chart and reward menu.

- Have parents introduce the program to their children and involve them in the process.

✎ Have parents start using the chart.

✎ Have parents bring the completed chart and reward menu to the next group.

✎ Remind parents to keep praising appropriate behavior and doing "one-on-one time" with their children.

CHAPTER 7

Session 5: Using Commands to Guide Children's Behavior

Session 5 Notes to Group Leaders

Overview

The first few sessions of the program have emphasized noticing, encouraging, and rewarding appropriate child behaviors through the use of praise, parental attention, and tangible rewards. This week, the program begins to focus on limit setting with preschoolers. The first step in effective limit setting is using effective commands. Thus, the goal of this session is to help parents use more effective commands.

Use of Commands

Research has shown that how one gives commands can greatly affect the likelihood of child compliance. In particular, commands have been shown to be more effective when they are clear and specific (Roberts, McMahon, Forehand, & Humphreys, 1978), phrased to tell a child what to do rather than what not to do (Houlihan & Jones, 1990), and given when the adult has eye contact with the child (Hamlet, Axelrod, & Kuerschner, 1984). Breaking down multistep commands into single-step commands allows parents to more easily follow through with consequences, and is particularly important with hyperactive preschoolers, who are likely to have short attention spans. Additionally, parents should be encouraged to avoid giving too many commands, because frequent commands are associated with less compliance in children (Forehand & Scarboro, 1975). Commands will be most effective if children know that parents are prepared to enforce them, so parents should only issue commands that they are prepared to enforce. Parents in the group will have different styles of giving commands. It will be important to help parents identify their own style to determine what specific changes they may need to make.

Commands versus Requests

Some parents may feel uncomfortable with the notion of giving "commands" because it seems impolite, and this may interfere with their ability to issue commands effectively. Therefore, it will be important to address this issue with parents and help them distinguish between commands and requests. Commands are typically in the form of a statement and should be used when it is important that a child comply with the parental directive, and when the parent has reason to believe that the command may not be obeyed. In contrast, requests are typically in the form of a question and can be used when compliance is optional. Parents should be encouraged to use both commands, to increase compliance, as well as requests, to model politeness.

Session 5 Curriculum

Materials Needed

- What is Your Style of Giving Commands? worksheet

- Effective Commands handout

- Command Flow Chart

- Commands Log

Outline

- Review homework from last session

- Introduce parents to commands, and have them complete the top portion of What is Your Style of Giving Commands? worksheet

- Review recommendations on how to phrase commands to make them more effective

- Review other things to keep in mind when giving commands

- Review the Command Flow Chart handout

- Have parents complete the bottom portion of the What is Your Style of Giving Commands? worksheet, and role-play the steps of the Command Flow Chart

- Assign homework

Homework Review

Review parents' completed charts and reward menus (approximately 15 minutes), and discuss any difficulties in using them.

Introduction to Commands

Introduce parents to the concept of using commands, using the following suggested script:

We have discussed the importance of noticing and rewarding children's appropriate behaviors through the use of praise, parental attention, and tangible rewards. However, it is also very important for parents to set limits on inappropriate behaviors. All children will test the limits you set. Through testing, children learn whether or not the rule is really a rule and whether or not you will be consistent. This can be a challenging time for parents of preschoolers. Using effective commands is an important step in helping you set limits.

Requests versus Commands

Tell the group that it is important to make a distinction between requests and commands, and think about when to use each of them.

Commands

- Commands are typically in the form of a statement. For example:

  - *"Please come here."*

  - *"Get in bed."*

- Advise parents to use commands in situations in which it is important that their children comply and in which they have some reason to believe that their children may not comply.

Requests

- Requests are typically in the form of a question and often involve polite language. For example:

  - *"Will you give that to me?"*

  - *"Would you please pass the salt?"*

- Note that using polite requests with a child teaches her how to be polite to others. Advise parents to use requests when compliance is optional or not particularly important. For example, they might *request* that a child pass the salt, but they would issue a *command* when they are telling a child to go to bed.

- Explain that today's session will focus on commands because they tend to be more challenging for parents.

In-Session Exercise: Command Style

Have parents complete the top portion of the What is Your Style of Giving Commands? worksheet. Discuss their responses.

How to Phrase Commands to Make Them More Effective

Review the following recommendations on how to phrase commands, referring group members to the Effective Commands handout.

Be Clear and Specific

- Parents should avoid vague commands (e.g., "Knock it off!," "Be good!"). For example:

  - *Instead of saying, "Anna be careful!" when Anna is sloshing her milk, say, "Anna use both hands to hold your glass," or, "Drink more slowly so you do not spill, please."*

- Parents should avoid saying "Let's" when they really want their children to do something by themselves. For example:

  - *Do not say, "Let's pick up your toys," when you mean, "Please pick up your toys."*

Avoid Questions

■ Parents should avoid phrasing a command/request as a question unless they are willing to accept no for an answer. For example:

> ■ *Rather than saying, "Do you want to pick up your toys now?" say, "Please pick up your toys now."*

Give Positive Directions

■ Parents should try to tell their children what *to do*, rather than what not to do. For example:

> ■ *Instead of saying, "Do not throw your coat on the floor," say, "Hang up your coat."*

> ■ *Instead of saying, "No running," say, "Walk, please."*

Give One Command at a Time

■ Parents should avoid stringing several commands together. Limiting commands to only one at a time is very important for hyperactive preschoolers. Preschoolers will not be able to remember all the parts in a multistep command, and parents will not be able to praise or use consequences when all those tasks are lumped together. For example:

> ■ *Instead of saying, "Go upstairs, brush your teeth, put on your pajamas, and get in bed," give only the first command: "Please go upstairs now." Once the child is upstairs, say, "Please put on your pajamas." After the pajamas are on, then tell the child to get in bed.*

Give Children Time to Comply

■ Encourage parents to wait for their children to comply rather than repeating themselves. If parents repeat their command over and over without any consequence for noncompliance, children learn that they do not really have to comply when given a command. For example:

> ■ *Say, "Come here," instead of, "Come here…come here…come here!"*

Other Things to Keep in Mind When Giving Commands

Review with the group other helpful suggestions for giving commands.

Keep Transition Times in Mind

- Track transitions and remind children when they are coming up. For example:

    - *"When this TV show is over, it will be time to pick up the toys." Then, when the show is over, "OK, the show is over, now please pick up your toys."*

- If a task can wait, give children some time to finish what they are doing.

Try to Reduce the Number of Commands

- Parents (of young hyperactive children especially) give many commands without even realizing it. The problem with giving so many commands is that it is difficult to follow each of those commands with consequences if a child does not comply. Here is a suggested script for discussing this with parents:

    - *Before you give a command, think about whether or not it is important and whether or not you are willing to follow through with a consequence (to be discussed in coming weeks) if your child does not comply or with praise if your child does comply. If you are not willing or able to follow up, or you decide that it really is not something that is so important after all, do not give the command.*

Command Flowchart

Review with the group the Command Flow Chart handout.

Get the Child's Attention Before Giving a Command

When giving a command with hyperactive preschoolers, it is critical to first get their attention.

- Encourage parents to avoid giving commands from another room—they should stand within 5 feet of their children if possible.

- Parents should remove distractions and not let their children distract them.

- Parents should keep eye contact with their children (but should not turn this into a battle if a child will not look at them, particularly if they know the child is paying attention to them).

- Sometimes it can be helpful to have the child repeat the command back to the parent to make sure she heard and understood.

State the Command

- Use a firm tone of voice.

- Use a matter-of-fact, businesslike tone, without yelling.

- It is fine to say *please* as long as it is part of a statement, not a question.

- Parents may pair their command with a brief reason, but they should be sure to keep it short or their children will start to tune them out. For example:

  - *"Please pick up your toys. I do not want anyone to step on them and break them or for anyone to get hurt."*

  - *"Hold my hand so we can be safe crossing the street."*

Wait 5 Seconds

- Encourage parents to count to 5 in their head while looking expectantly at their children. If the child complies, parents can praise the child. If the child does not comply, parents can give a warning. For example:

  - *"If you do not put your blocks away now, I will put them away and you will not play with them tomorrow." Wait another 5 seconds, and then if she does not comply, follow through with a consequence; if she does comply, follow through with praise.*

- Sometimes it can be helpful for parents to give their children a time frame for when compliance is expected before a consequence is given. For example:

  - *"You need to start brushing your teeth by the time I count to five or we will not be able to read a story tonight." Then start counting out loud.*

- Sometimes parents count without giving a specific consequence of what will happen if the child does not comply by the time the parent reaches a certain number. Discourage parents from doing this.

In-Session Exercise: Working on Command Style

Have parents identify what they would like to work on when giving commands, completing the bottom portion of the What is Your Style of Giving Commands? worksheet.

Next role-play (in small groups) one or more of the situations on the worksheet, following the steps of the Command Flow Chart.

Homework

✎ Have parents practice using more effective commands at home.

✎ Have parents pick a 20-minute period sometime this week when they are with their children. Ask them to notice whenever they give their children a command during those 20 minutes, and write down those commands on the Commands Log.

✎ Have parents bring their completed Commands Logs with them to the next session for discussion.

CHAPTER 8

Session 6: Using Logical and Natural Consequences and Rewards

Session 6 Notes to Group Leaders

Overview

Last session, parents learned how to make their commands more effective. In this session, group leaders begin to discuss strategies for when a child misbehaves or does not comply with a parental command. As discussed in Session 2, when something pleasant follows a behavior, the behavior is more likely to occur in the future (reinforcement), whereas when something unpleasant follows a behavior, the behavior is less likely to occur in the future (punishment). Using these principles, this session will focus on using consequences to discourage inappropriate behavior and using rewards to encourage appropriate behavior. In particular, the goal for this session is to teach parents about logical and natural consequences and rewards and to help them begin to use these at home over the next week.

Effectiveness of Consequences

The use of negative consequences with young children has been shown to significantly decrease noncompliance (Little & Kelley, 1989), including in children who are hyperactive (Rosen, O'Leary, Joyce, Conway, & Pfiffner, 1984). In fact, simply warning children about negative consequences increases the likelihood that they will comply (Owen, Smith Slep, & Heyman, 2009). However, it is critical that consequences are delivered in a firm and consistent manner. Use of overly harsh consequences, as well as failure to consistently employ consequences for child misbehavior, have been associated with problematic child behavior (Baumrind & Black, 1967; Baumrind, 1966). Thus, it is critical to teach parents how to use consequences effectively.

Challenges of Instituting Consequences

Parents may be particularly concerned about how children will react when a parent tries to give a consequence for a misbehavior that has not received a consequence in the past. In fact, parents should be prepared for children to be very unhappy and perhaps initially escalate in their misbehavior before realizing that there has been a shift in parenting. It is important to talk with parents about how critical it is to follow through so that the child does not learn that he can get out of a consequence by engaging in further misbehavior. In this situation it can be easy for parents and children to fall into a coercive cycle (Patterson, 2002). Parents may either find themselves escalating, resulting in overly harsh discipline (which will likely get rewarded by the child's compliance), or giving in (which will reward the child's negative behavior).

Effectiveness of Rewards

Session 4 focused on rewards, so the primary emphasis in this session is on the use of negative consequences. However, consequences can often be framed either as negative consequences or as positive rewards, and parents are encouraged to use the latter whenever possible. This session extends what parents learned in session 4 and emphasizes the use of logical and natural rewards that can be used outside of rewards systems.

Session 6 Curriculum

Materials Needed

- Natural and Logical Consequences and Rewards handout
- Consequences and Rewards worksheet
- Consequences and Rewards Log

Outline

- Review homework from last session

- Introduce the use of consequences and rewards

- Present ways to make consequences and rewards more effective

- Discuss how to deliver consequences and rewards effectively

- Review other things to keep in mind when using consequences and rewards

- Conduct in-session exercises to generate consequences and rewards and role-play using them effectively

- Assign homework

Homework Review

Review homework from last session (approximately 10 minutes). Discuss any difficulties using more effective commands and review completed Commands Log.

Introduction to Consequences and Rewards

Introduce the use of consequences and rewards using the following suggested script:

Today we will talk about how to use consequences and rewards to help your child behave. Because hyperactive children have difficulty putting the brakes on their own behavior, consequences can be a very powerful tool for helping them put the brakes on their behavior. Hyperactive children are very sensitive to immediate feedback from their environment, and if we set up their environment in the right way, we can help them function better in their daily lives.

Explain that there are different types of consequences and rewards they will be learning to use. Refer parents to the Natural and Logical Consequences and Rewards handout.

Natural Consequences and Rewards

Explain that natural consequences and rewards follow naturally from a child's actions if parents do not intervene.

- If a child breaks his toy, the natural consequence is that he can no longer have that toy.

- If a child shares his toy with another child, the natural reward is that the other child might be more likely to share with him.

Logical Consequences and Rewards

Explain logical consequences and rewards as those that are tied to the misbehavior (in the case of consequences) or appropriate behavior (in the case of rewards) in a logical way.

- If a child writes on the wall with crayons, the logical consequence might be not being able to use the crayons for the rest of the day.

- If a child gets ready for bed quickly, the logical reward might be that he gets an extra story before turning out the light.

Discussion: Natural and Logical Consequences and Rewards at Home

Note that not all consequences and rewards have to be natural or logical, but, if they are, it may be easier for a child to understand the link between his behavior and the consequence of that behavior and easier for parents to follow through.

To open up discussion, ask group members the following:

- *What types of natural consequences and rewards have you tried using at home?*

- *What types of logical consequences and rewards have you tried using at home?*

- *What has worked and what has not worked?*

Ways to Make Consequences and Rewards More Effective

Review the following guidelines, referring group members to the Natural and Logical Consequences and Rewards handout.

Choosing Consequences and Rewards

Make it Meaningful

Emphasize the importance of making consequences and rewards meaningful and discuss examples.

- Consequences that are *not* meaningful:

  - *"If you throw food on the floor again, you will not be able to have extra broccoli."*

  - *"If you keep whining, we are going to leave the grocery store."*

- Consequences that *are* meaningful:

  - *"If you throw food again, you will not have dessert."*

  - *"You cannot watch TV until you clean up your Legos."*

- Rewards that are *not* meaningful:

  - *"If you hurry up, we can get to preschool on time."*

- Rewards that *are* meaningful

  - *"If you get ready for bed quickly, we can read an extra story."*

  - *"If you eat your vegetables, you can have dessert."*

Avoid Overly Harsh and Long-Term Consequences

Consequences should not be overly harsh or punitive. Explain that the idea of consequences is to help children learn what behavior is acceptable and what is not. Consequences are a tool for helping children learn—the punishment need not fit the crime.

- This sometimes means that a child may have the same consequence for a minor misbehavior as he has for a serious misbehavior.

- Parents should not take away a toy for a month or indefinitely. This may make a child angry and resentful, and the original misbehavior will be long forgotten by the child after a month. It is also more difficult to enforce a long-term consequence. Instead, parents should take away a toy or privilege for 24 hours, or the rest of the day. By removing privileges for just 24 hours, parents also will have a new supply of privileges to remove the next day if necessary.

In-Session Exercise: Generating Consequences and Rewards

Have parents complete the Consequences and Reward worksheet in which they generate a list of rewards and consequences they will use at home.

Delivering Consequences and Rewards Effectively

Be Immediate

Emphasize that consequences and rewards should be as immediate as possible. This is critical for hyperactive preschoolers, who are particularly focused on the short-term. If the consequence or reward is delayed, it will not be as powerful.

Follow Through

Advise parents to not threaten a consequence or offer a reward that they cannot or would not carry out.

- Examples of empty threats:

    - *Threatening to leave a child behind somewhere if he is dawdling.*

    - *Threatening to take away a family event (like going on vacation).*

- Examples of empty promises:

    - *Telling a child he might get to go to Disney World if he sleeps in his own bed for a month.*

    - *Telling a child you might buy him an expensive toy if he behaves well.*

If parents catch themselves making empty threats or promises, it is fine to correct themselves. For example:

- *"I just told you that I would leave you here if you do not come and I should not have said that, because I would never leave you somewhere alone. If you do not come with me now, you will not be able to watch any TV for the rest of the day."*

Be Consistent

Emphasize that it is important to give the consequence every time the target misbehavior occurs.

Be Straightforward and Assertive

Encourage parents to be matter-of-fact in delivering consequences.

- Try to ignore a child's protests or pleading.

- Try not to lecture or criticize. Parents can give a brief explanation and then let the experience of the consequence speak for itself. For example:

    - *"You may not play with your crayons until tomorrow because you wrote on the wall."*

- Parents do not need to offer an apology after giving a consequence.

Other Things to Keep in Mind When Using Consequences and Rewards

A Fresh Start

Once a child has been given a consequence, encourage parents to give the child a new opportunity to be successful. Give children a chance to do things differently next time and praise them if they do.

Expect Limit-Testing

Tell parents to expect their children to test the limits. This will be particularly true if they have not been consistent with consequences in the past. Their children may purposely disobey to see if parents will follow through with a consequence.

It is also not uncommon for children to throw temper tantrums when given a consequence. This will be discussed in detail in later sessions, but in the meantime give the following tips for handling tantrums:

- Be empathic but stay firm. Parents can remind themselves that this is part of children's learning.

- If parents anticipate that the child is going to be very upset about a consequence, it is sometimes helpful to say something like the following after parents have given a warning:

  - *"If you do not start getting dressed by the time I count to five, we will not be able to read any stories tonight. One. Two. Three."* If the child does not comply, the parent should come close to the child and say very calmly and quietly the following: *"You have a choice right now. You can cooperate and we can read stories. Or you can not cooperate and you will lose your stories and you will probably be very sad about it. It is your choice. Think about it for a second."* Parents should then wait a couple of seconds and then continue counting.

- Parents should not change their minds about a consequence once they have given it no matter how big the tantrum. If they hold firm, the child will learn that he cannot get out of a consequence by whining, complaining, or having a tantrum.

Consider Rewards

Remind parents that they often have a choice between removing a privilege and giving a reward. Whenever possible, parents should state what appropriate behavior they want to see and state what the reward is for engaging in that behavior. For example:

- *Instead of saying, "If you keep standing up in your chair, you cannot have dessert," say, "If you keep your bottom on your chair until we are finished eating, then you can have dessert."*

Back Each Other Up

Stress that when using rewards and consequences it is important for parents to back each other up. Unless parents believe that a consequence or reward that another parent has imposed is harmful or dangerous, they should back them up even if it is not what they would have done.

When Children Still Do Not Comply after a Consequence

If a parent gives a consequence and the child still does not do what he is supposed to, advise parents to do one of two things depending on the situation:

- Gently but firmly make the child comply (while still implementing the consequence). For example:

  - *Pick your child up and gently but firmly put your child in the car or in bed or at the dinner table.*

- Drop the subject and let the consequence stand. For example:

  - *Your child does not pick up his toys and loses TV for the rest of the day. The toys stay on the floor until the next day, or you can pick them up knowing that your child has been punished for not picking up.*

In-Session Exercise: Role-Playing

Role-play giving consequences and rewards in small groups following the Natural and Logical Consequences and Rewards handout.

Homework

✎ Have parents practice using consequences and rewards at home when their children misbehave.

✎ Have parents use the Consequences and Rewards Log to record some of the consequences and rewards for misbehavior. Parents should identify whether it was a natural or logical consequence or reward and record their children's and their own reactions. Ask them to review their logs before the next session and think about how it went to use consequences and rewards over the course of the week—what worked well and what was difficult?

✎ Have parents bring their completed logs to the next session for discussion.

Session 7 Notes to Group Leaders

Overview

Time out is short for "time out from reinforcement" and, like other strategies taught in this program, is also based on learning principles. When children engage in undesirable behaviors, removing them from fun activities and the attention of others (which is highly reinforcing for most children) just for a few minutes will typically decrease the likelihood that the child engages in that behavior again (the term for this is *negative punishment*, although we advise against introducing this technical term). Many studies have shown time out to be effective with young children, and time out provides parents with a method of punishment that is thought to be safer both physically and emotionally compared to many other forms of punishment (i.e., spanking) to which parents often resort (Morawska & Sanders, 2010). This program presents time out after first teaching parents strategies that promote a nurturing parent–child relationship and that focus on rewarding appropriate behavior, because time out is thought to be most effective in the context of a warm and supportive relationship (Morawska & Sanders, 2010). Encouraging parents to use other tools first before resorting to time out also helps to prevent parents from overusing it.

Use of Time Out for Hyperactive Children

When giving time out to a hyperactive child, it is important to emphasize that parents may need to adjust their method of time out to accommodate their children's difficulty sitting still. For example, the use of a time out chair may not be ideal for a hyperactive preschooler because sitting still in the chair may simply not be feasible. Designating a time out area may be preferable. Parents must have realistic expectations for their children's behavior during time out, or time out can backfire.

Criticisms of Time Out

Parents likely come to the program with preconceived ideas about time out. Some parents may have had good experiences, whereas others may have found time out to be ineffective. For parents who have not had good experiences with time out, it may be helpful to remind them that very small modifications in the way that time out is delivered can make a difference in its effectiveness. Parents may also have heard criticisms of time out in the media, from other parents, or from educators. It is therefore important to be aware of the debate about time out. Critics of time out have argued that this approach does not help children develop alternative strategies, can harm their self-confidence, and can be confusing for children (Gartrell, 2001). Much of the criticism of time out has centered around the use of time out in school settings, where children may feel embarrassed in front of their peers. It may be useful to help parents understand the distinction between using time out in the privacy of their own homes and having a child be given a time out in front of her entire class. It may also be helpful to emphasize that there is no evidence that time out is harmful for children when it is carried out properly, and that there is ample evidence that it is quite effective in reducing aggressive and disruptive behaviors in children (Morawska & Sanders, 2010), including children who experience difficulties with hyperactivity (Fabiano et al., 2004).

Session 7 Curriculum

Materials Needed

- Time Out handout

- Time Out Step-by-Step handout

- Time Out Log

Outline

■ Review homework from last session

■ Introduce time out, including when it should be used, what is needed, how long it should be, and where it should be

■ Review what to do at the start of time out, during time out, and at the end of time out

■ Review common problems that can occur in time out

■ Review other guidelines for an effective time out

■ Role-play a time out

■ Assign homework

Homework Review

Review parents' Consequences and Rewards Logs (approximately 10–15 minutes). Discuss successes and difficulties with using consequences and rewards over the past week.

Introduction to Time Out

Introduce time out using the following suggested script:

Time out stands for "time out from reinforcement." It is designed to remove positives rather than introducing negatives. Time out is most effective if you continue to use positive attention with your children. If your child is not receiving enough positive attention, the time out session may be rewarding for your child because she gets at least a little attention for a few minutes.

Time out is different from "taking space" to calm down. Time out is a punishment for misbehavior. Taking space to calm down is a great technique for handling strong feelings (which will be discussed more in later sessions).

Review the following recommendations, referring parents to the Time Out handout.

When Should Time Out Be Used?

Explain that time out should be used for more severe behaviors, such as aggression or destruction. It is important not to overuse time out, so parents should select the behaviors they are most concerned about.

Have parents choose which misbehaviors will be targeted for time out.

What is Needed for Time Out?

To implement time out, parents will need the following:

- A quiet, boring area of the house (see below)

- A timer

- A list of backup consequences. For example:

  - *No more TV for the day*

  - *No dessert*

  - *Removal of a favorite toy for the day*

Backup consequences should involve losing specific privileges for that day (consequences should not involve removal of privileges beyond today unless it is late enough in the day that there are no more privileges to remove, in which case parents can remove a privilege for the next day). Parents should make sure that it is a privilege that their children care about.

In-Session Exercise: Choosing Consequences

Have parents decide on their backup consequences.

How Long Should Time Out Be?

Inform the group that time out does not need to be long to be effective, and there are many advantages to having it shorter, including the fact that it will be easier for parents to do it correctly. Time out ideally should be one to three minutes for preschoolers. For a hyperactive preschooler, three minutes will seem like an eternity for both parent and child.

Where Should Time Out Be?

Time out can be in any quiet place where there is nothing that is entertaining (for example, not near the television if it is on). Although chairs or couches are common choices for time out, a hyperactive preschooler may not be able to remain seated, so it may be helpful to choose a different location for time out. If parents use a couch or chair as the location for the time out, their expectation should be that the child remains near the couch or chair during time out, rather than expecting the child to sit still.

- **Examples of Where to Have Time Out**

  - *The bottom of the stairs*

  - *An empty area of a room* (parents can use tape to mark off the area if that is helpful)

  - *A hallway*

  - *A couch or chair* (though a chair is likely to be too confining for a hyperactive preschooler)

- **Examples of Where to Avoid Having Time Out**

  - *A child's room* (There are typically entertaining things in children's rooms. It is also easy for a parent to forget about a child when using the child's room for time out, and time out ends up being too long.)

  - *Near a television that is on*

  - *Near toys or other people who may talk to the child*

  - *Any place that is potentially dangerous or frightening for the child—no bathrooms, basements, or closets*

In-Session Exercise: Choosing Location

Have parents decide on their time out location.

Time Out Procedure

Review how to start time out, what to do during time out, and how to end time out. Again, refer parents to the Time Out handout.

How to Start Time Out?

Review the following steps.

1. Go near the child and say, "You may not _____. You need to go to time out."

2. Bring the child to the time out area (walk with or carry the child there). If the child refuses to go to the time out area, say, "If you do

not go to time out by the time I count to five, you will not be able to _____" (name a backup consequence). If the child still does not go to time out, tell her that she has lost the privilege that was mentioned as the backup consequence, and end the time out. Depending on what the privilege removal is, parents can try one more backup consequence: "Okay, no more TV for the day. Now if you do not go to time out, you will also lose dessert today." If the child still does not go to time out, that is the end of time out. Give no more than two backup consequences.

3. If the child goes to the time out area, say in a businesslike voice, "You need to stay in this area until the timer beeps. I cannot talk to you during time out, but will talk to you after time out. When the timer beeps, if you are quiet, you can get out of time out." (Once the child understands how time out works, these instructions can be dropped.)

4. Set the timer and make sure that the child knows it is being set.

In-Session Exercise: Role-Play

Have parents break up into pairs and role-play the first phase of time out (i.e., telling the child they need to go to time out and bringing the child to time out).

What Should Parents Do During Time Out?

Give parents the following general suggestions.

- Monitor the child to make sure that she stays in the time out area. Stay close enough to keep an eye on the child, but not so close that it feels like company.

- Avoid looking directly at the child during time out. Use peripheral vision to make sure that the child is in the correct area.

- Avoid talking to the child during time out, and keep other family members from talking to the child.

How to End Time Out

Review how to end time out:

- When the timer beeps, if the child is quiet (i.e., not screaming), say, "You can get out of time out now."

- At this point, if it is appropriate, parents can have a more detailed conversation with the child about why her behavior is not appropriate, and work on resolving whatever situation led up to the misbehavior. It is also fine to drop the topic and move on.

Common Problems That Can Occur in Time Out

To help parents anticipate common problems, review the following guidelines.

What to Do If The Child Leaves the Time Out Area

Review with parents the following steps:

1. Tell the child, "You need to get back in the time out area."

2. If the child does not get back in the time out area say, "If you do not get back in the time out area, you will lose (name the backup consequence)."

3. If the child still does not go back into the time out area say, "You did not go back into time out, so (name the backup consequence)." Then time out ends.

4. If it helps to make clear what the punishment was for the behavior (if the child did not complete the time out), parents can repeat the behavior and backup consequence. For example: "You hit me, and I do not allow hitting, so now you will not be able to watch TV for the rest of the day."

Note that sometimes parents feel like they have "lost" if the child does not end up serving the time out. Stress to parents that it is important to remember that the backup consequence is the punishment for the misbehavior (and it is often a worse punishment than the time out itself). This is not the time for power struggles; it is a time for the child to learn that misbehaviors have consequences.

What to Do If the Child Screams/Has a Temper Tantrum During Time Out

Give parents the following guidelines:

- Ignore the screaming or tantrumming unless the timer has beeped, in which case parents can remind the child that she needs to be quiet to get out of time out. Parents can remind the child every 5 minutes that she needs to be quiet to get out of time out.

- Hyperactive children are often louder and more talkative than other children, so parents may need to be flexible about this rule. If the child has been in time out for 15 minutes, parents can start lowering their expectations for how long the child needs to be quiet to get out of time out.

In-Session Exercise: Role-Play

Have parents break up into pairs and role-play the child leaving time out and not being quiet during time out.

What to Do If the Child Acts Out or Pretends to Like Time Out

Advise simply ignoring certain types of behavior during time out:

- If the child swears or says mean and horrible things during time out, ignore it!

- If the child dances, sings, or talks about how much she likes being in time out, ignore it! Just because a child acts like she likes time out does not mean she does!

Other Guidelines for Time Out

Review the following additional guidelines for time out.

Giving Warnings for Time Out

Note that for misbehavior that does not involve aggression and destruction, parents can give a warning for time out. Parents should give only one warning, and be prepared to follow through!

Giving Time Out in Public

Advise that parents wait until time out is well established in their own homes before attempting to give time out in public. For time out in public:

- Simply find the quietest, most boring place possible. For example:

  - *In the car* (parents should make sure they are in the car or just outside of the car with the child). IMPORTANT NOTE: Only use this location if it is not too hot or too cold in the car.

- *Outside a store against a boring wall.* The child does not need to face the wall—the goal is not to shame the child. Simply designate a location where the child needs to stand.

Importance of Parents Staying Calm During Time Out

Emphasize that time out will be most effective if parents can stay calm and businesslike during the time out. If they are yelling and emotional or warm and nurturing during time out, the time out may not be effective.

In-Session Exercise: Role-Play

Have parents break into pairs and role-play time out from start to finish. Refer parents to the Time Out Step-by-Step handout.

Homework

- Have parents try time out at home and record what happened on the Time Out Log.

  - If parents have never used time out, it may help to explain to the child what will happen before the child misbehaves. For example:

    - *"I do not like it when you hit me, so from now on, whenever you hit me, you will have to go to time out for 3 minutes. Here is where you will have your time out. I will not be able to talk to you while you are in time out. If you get out of time out, then you will (tell them the backup consequence)."*

  - If parents have used time out before but it has been very different from this program's use of it, then they should explain to the child how it will be different.

CHAPTER 10

Session 8: Teaching Children Problem-Solving and Negotiating Skills

Session 8 Notes to Group Leaders

Overview

The preschool years are an important time for the development of problem-solving and negotiating skills (Klimes-Dougan & Kopp, 1999). Children tend to be more socially and behaviorally well-adjusted when they have stronger social problem-solving abilities (Raikes, Virmani, Thompson, & Hatton, 2013) and negotiation skills (Yeates, Schultz, & Selman, 1991). Although preschoolers' ability to engage in problem solving and negotiating is still rudimentary, nurturing these skills in young children can provide them with the tools they will need to successfully meet life's challenges. Moreover, there is clear evidence that actively teaching children problem-solving and negotiating skills helps boost their effective use of these skills (Bierman et al., 2008).

Children who are hyperactive tend to face frequent challenges, and problem solving and negotiating may be important tools for helping to meet these challenges. However, children who are hyperactive tend to have greater difficulty engaging effectively in negotiating (Normand et al., 2013) and social problem solving (Matthys, Cuperus, & Van Engeland, 1999). Thus, fostering these skills early in development in hyperactive preschoolers may be key for their social development.

Problem Solving and Negotiating as Program Tools

Like most of the tools in this program, problem solving and negotiating should be used in moderation. Discussions that foster the development of these skills in children can take time. If a parent attempts to engage in these discussions every time there is a conflict, not only could this be all-consuming but also it could run the risk of inadvertently teaching children that engaging in conflict is an effective tool for getting a parent's attention. Also keep in mind that some preschoolers already have an extremely well-developed set of negotiating skills that they turn to any time they fail to get what they want. In these cases, parents should encourage their children to use these skills in moderation.

Parents vary considerably in the degree to which they value teaching children problem solving and negotiating. This session may not resonate with parents who place a high value on teaching children to respect authority. It is important to respect parents' different values and not push them to use tools that they are not comfortable with. However, group leaders can encourage a discussion of the benefits of teaching the skills and can work with parents to evaluate whether they can incorporate these tools in a manner that is consistent with their parenting values.

Proactive Parenting

This session ends with a discussion of proactive parenting—how parents can anticipate problems that are likely to occur and avoid or minimize these difficulties. This discussion can focus on using proactive parenting across all of the tools that have been presented so far, though it lends itself particularly well to problem solving. Engaging in this discussion before entering the emotion socialization portion of this program is useful because preparing for upsetting situations can often make them less challenging. As the group begins discussing emotional situations in upcoming sessions, it may be useful to revisit this notion of proactive parenting.

Session 8 Curriculum

Materials Needed

- Teaching Problem Solving and Negotiating handout
- Teaching Problem Solving and Negotiating Log

Outline

- Review homework from last session

- Introduce problem solving

- Present guidelines for using problem solving with children and conduct role-playing exercise

- Present guidelines for teaching negotiating to children and conduct role-playing exercise

- Introduce and discuss concept of proactive parenting

- Assign homework

Homework Review

Review parents' completed Time Out Logs (approximately 15–20 minutes). Have parents share how things went using time out over the last week.

Introduction to Problem Solving

Introduce problem solving using the following suggested script:

One of the most important things that preschoolers are learning is how to solve problems. Preschool children, particularly hyperactive preschool children, face many challenges over the course of the day. It can be very tempting for parents to step in and solve problems for children, but if you use these challenges as opportunities to teach your child how to solve problems you will not only help your child develop an important skill, you will also ultimately make your job easier by teaching your child how to face his own challenges.

Benefits of Teaching Problem Solving to Children

Getting in the habit of using problem solving when parents and children have a problem can have benefits as children get older and problem solving becomes an important tool for handling conflict.

Using Problem Solving in Moderation

Problem solving is a great tool to use when children are upset about something. Parents should not use problem solving every time a child is unhappy—there are many times when parents need to set a limit without discussion. Use this for problems that are likely to have good compromise solutions.

Keep It Short

Hyperactive children are not likely to be able to engage in long problem-solving sessions, so be brief and to the point.

Using Problem Solving With Children

Review the following procedure for using problem solving with children.

Define the Problem

Tell parents that in order to solve a problem they and their children need to be clear about what the problem is. Even if they think they know what the problem is, it is important to state it out loud. Give the following guidelines, referring parents to the Teaching Problem Solving and Negotiating handout.

- When parents have a problem-solving session with their children, they should get down on their children's level, establish eye contact, and make sure that they have their children's full attention.

- Parents can start by asking the child what the problem is. They should try to use a calm, noncritical tone of voice. For example:

  - *"What is the problem?"*

  - *"What is making you so upset?"*

- If the child is too upset to be able to state the problem, parents can define the problem themselves or state what they think the problem is, and ask the child if it is correct. For example:

  - *"It looks like you're unhappy because your brother is playing with something you want. Is that right?"*

  - *"Are you upset because I told you that you can't watch another TV show?"*

- Remind parents that they do not have to agree with the child that there is a legitimate problem. They just have to be able to help the child describe the problem from his perspective.

100

- If there are two children involved and they have two different perspectives, it is important to state the problem from each child's perspective. For example:

  - *"It seems like the problem is that Matthew really wants to play with the toy that Jacob is playing with, because Jacob has been playing with it for a while, but Jacob feels like it should be his turn because he was playing with it first."*

- If the conflict is between the parent and child, and they have two different perspectives on the problem, the problem should be stated from both points of view. For example:

  - *"So you want to stay longer at the playground, but I need to get home to cook dinner."*

Help Children Generate Solutions to the Problem

The next step is to ask, "How can we solve this problem?" Review with parents the following steps in this process:

- Encourage parents to wait to see if the child has ideas. If the child expresses an idea, parents can simply restate the idea so that the child knows that the parent heard him. Parents should not criticize the ideas yet. Parents may even be surprised how good the child's solutions are!

- If the child has a good idea, parents should congratulate the child on coming up with a solution, and implement it. Encourage parents to really make a big deal of this. If the idea just needs a few modifications, parents can suggest changes.

- If the child is not able to come up with any reasonable solutions, parents can suggest several of their own.

- Once they have generated a few reasonable ideas, parents can ask the child which idea he likes best. If the child likes a reasonable option, even if it is not the parents' favorite option, parents should agree to his choice to help him gain confidence in the problem-solving process. If he likes an idea that does not seem reasonable, parents can say what they like about the idea, but then explain why they think the idea will not work.

Note that children may not be actively involved at first. At first parents may simply be modeling the problem-solving process for them.

In-Session Exercise: Role-Play

Use the following scenario for role-play:

Your child has a friend over to play. You hear them screaming at each other and go in to investigate. They are both holding the same toy and insisting that it is their turn to play with it.

Divide into groups of three, and have two people pretend to be the child and one person the parent who is going to help them problem-solve.

Teaching Good Negotiating Skills

Explain that part of the problem-solving process involves being able to negotiate and compromise. Review the following guidelines, referring parents to the Teaching Problem Solving and Negotiating handout.

Disagreements with Other Children

- If a child is having a disagreement with another child, parents can give the child suggestions of things he can say to negotiate a solution. For example:

  - *"Maybe you could ask John if you can have a turn in 5 minutes."*

  - *"Do you want to bring this toy to John to see if he would like to trade?"*

Negotiating with Parents

- Teaching children to negotiate with parents can be a great way for them to practice negotiating. Clearly there are many issues that are nonnegotiable, but children may more easily accept these nonnegotiables if there are some issues on which there is room for negotiation. For example:

  - *You tell your child it is time to go to bed, and he starts whining and complaining. You might say, "Whining and complaining are not good ways to get what you want. You have to go to bed soon, but you could try asking me in a nice voice if you can stay up for 5 more minutes." If your child does this, you should say something like, "I like how you asked me in a nice voice, so okay. But after 5 minutes you really have to go to bed." (And make sure to follow through on this!)*

Discussion: Identifying Negotiable Situations

To open up discussion regarding which situations are negotiable and which are not, ask the following:

- *What types of situations might be good to use negotiation?*

- *What types of situations are nonnegotiable?*

Nonnegotiable Issues

- Point out that when parents come across issues that are nonnegotiable (and there are many of these!) and their children are upset about it, it may help for parents to put it in the larger context. For example:

  - *You might say, "You do not get to decide everything, but I do try to let you decide as many things as I can." Remind your child of some of the times when he did have a choice and when you were willing to go along with his suggestion. Then move on gently but firmly.*

Whining and Complaining

- It is important that children start to learn to get things by asking nicely and negotiating rather than by whining and complaining. However, since most preschoolers will naturally respond by whining and complaining when they do not get their way, parents must gradually teach their children more appropriate behavior. At first, this means letting children's polite requests and negotiations "work" even if they were directly prompted by parents and they came after whining and complaining.

- As children begin to learn to ask nicely and negotiate, parents can raise the bar by having the polite request and negotiations "work" only if they were not preceded by whining and complaining.

In-Session Exercise: Role-Play

Have parents role-play one of the situations that was identified during the group discussion about situations that are negotiable. During this role-play, children should initially be defiant, and parents should coach children to use negotiation.

Proactive Parenting

Explain that one important part of parenting involves anticipating situations that are likely to be challenging and taking steps to prevent or minimize problems. Tell parents that they can use the tools discussed in this program to prevent problems as well as to handle problems once they occur.

Preventing Problems

In many cases, problems occur consistently in the same types of situations. For example, getting ready for school/daycare in the morning, going to bed, and going shopping are common situations that are difficult for preschoolers.

If parents can identify these difficult situations and have conversations with their preschooler when they are not in the heat of the moment, they can sometimes ward off problems.

Review the following examples of how parents can prevent problems.

Problem-Solve in Advance

- For situations that a child regularly has difficulty with, parents can try to include him in problem solving. For example:

  - *"Getting ready in the mornings has been really hard. I wonder if we can figure out how to solve this problem?"*

- Even if a specific solution is not identified, just talking about it may help a child try harder.

Remind Children about Expectations and Consequences/Rewards

- In advance of problem situations, parents can discuss expectations for behavior with their children as well as consequences for bad behavior and rewards for good behavior. If a parent starts the conversation with a positive statement about the child, it may be received better. For example:

  - *"We are going to the grocery store and I really like shopping with you when you cooperate. So remember, there is no screaming in the grocery store and you need to stay in the grocery cart. If you can cooperate, you can choose one small thing for us to buy at the end of the trip."*

■ *"You are such a good friend to Charlie, but I have noticed that sometimes when he comes over you get kind of wild. If I see that happen, I am going to ask you to stop, and if you do not stop, I am going to have to separate you for a little while."*

Discussion: Preventing Problems

To open up discussion, ask group members the following questions:

■ *What are some situations that are often challenging for your child, and your child has a difficult time following rules or is very likely to get upset?*

■ *And what are some steps you might be able to take ahead of time to make these situations less difficult?*

To end this discussion, the following script may be used:

As we move into our next part of the program, when we talk more about children's emotional development, it will be important to keep in mind these tools for preventing problems. One of the best ways of managing emotions is to think ahead about upsetting situations and change the way we think about them or approach them. Using this approach with your children will not only teach them an important skill for managing their emotions, but will decrease the number of challenging situations you and your children face.

Homework

✎ Have parents complete the Teaching Problem Solving and Negotiating Log, recording two problem-solving situations with their children. One situation should involve something that comes up spontaneously, and the other should involve a problem that happens frequently and that parents will talk with the child about ahead of time.

CHAPTER 11

Session 9: Learning About Emotion Development

Session 9 Notes to Group Leaders

Overview

Acquiring emotional competence is presumed to be a major developmental task for preschoolers (Supplee et al., 2011) and involves three interdependent components: emotion knowledge/understanding (the ability to identify one's own and others' emotions), emotion expression (verbal or nonverbal communication of emotions), and emotion regulation (the ability to manage or change one's emotions and expression of emotions; Denham et al., 2008). Children who are hyperactive have been shown to experience difficulty with each of these aspects of emotional competence (Cadesky, Mota, & Schachar, 2000; Sinzig, Morsch, & Lehmkuhl, 2008; Walcott & Landau, 2004; Williams et al., 2008). There are number of ways parents can foster their children's emotional competence and development, including but not limited to labeling emotions, validating emotions, and modeling healthy emotion expression. Thus, over the course of the next six sessions, this program emphasizes teaching parents emotion socialization skills to help their preschoolers develop better emotion competence. The main goals of session 9 are to provide psychoeducation about emotional development and help parents reflect on their own beliefs, values, and goals about emotions.

Psychoeducation on Emotional Development

Providing parents with information about emotional development will lay an important foundation for using the emotion socialization practices that will be taught in this program. Viewing emotions as a normal and adaptive part of life can make it easier for parents to validate children's emotions, which is one of the most important goals of this program. For example, understanding that babies universally experience several basic emotions from birth, and by 6 months of age can experience many emotions, including joy, fear, anger, disgust, and sadness (Lewis, 2008), illustrates that emotion is a core part of human experience. In addition, engaging parents in a discussion about the ways in which our basic emotions are adaptive—even seemingly negative ones—can help parents shift away from viewing negative emotions as something to squelch.

It is important not only to help parents understand that children experience emotions from a very young age, but also to gain insight into why children have difficulty regulating their emotions. A very basic description of the biological reasons for this can be helpful. The amygdala, the part of the brain that plays a key role in producing emotions, is already formed at birth (Tottenham, 2012), which explains why infants can experience emotions right away. However, other parts of the brain that are essential for controlling emotions, such as the prefrontal cortex, are not well developed early in life (Tottenham, 2012). As a child ages and the prefrontal cortex develops, the child will naturally become better at regulating emotions. Thus, preschoolers may exhibit difficulties regulating emotions because the areas of the brain responsible for regulating emotions are less developed than areas of the brain responsible for producing emotions. And, unfortunately, preschoolers who are hyperactive may be even more vulnerable to these difficulties due to dysfunction in the prefrontal cortex (Barkley, 1997).

Parents' Own Experiences and Goals

In addition to providing parents with psychoeducation about emotional development, it is important to explore parents' own experiences regarding emotions. Parents' beliefs, values, and goals are critical for shaping parenting practices (Darling & Steinberg, 1993). Parents have received many explicit and implicit messages about emotions throughout their lives that likely impact their emotion socialization practices. Help parents consider the messages they received when they were young, and think about the messages they would like to teach to their children about emotions and emotion expression. This awareness can help parents engage in practices that are in keeping with their emotion socialization goals. It may also help parents to avoid using practices to which they automatically turn, based on their own early experiences, but that are inconsistent with the lessons they wish to teach their own children.

Materials Needed

- Emotion Development in Children handout

- Brain Development and Emotion handout

- Emotion Beliefs, Values, and Goals worksheet

- Emotion Log

Outline

- Review homework from last session

- Introduce the concept of emotion regulation and its relation to emotional competence

- Discuss brain development and cognitive abilities that help regulate emotion

- Encourage parents to respect their children's emotional experiences

- Discuss parents' values, beliefs, and goals about emotion expression

- Review some factors that are thought to foster emotional development and competence

- Assign homework

Homework Review

Review parents' completed logs on the Teaching Problem Solving and Negotiating worksheet (approximately 10 minutes). Discuss any difficulties in using problem solving and negotiation.

Introduction to Emotion Regulation

Introduce the concept of emotion regulation using the following suggested script:

Over the next six sessions, we will be talking about ways that you can help your child develop good emotion regulation skills. This is particularly important for hyperactive preschool children, because they tend to have more difficulty with emotion regulation. Some of the things that we have already talked about are important to your child's emotional development, such as providing praise and positive attention, so we want you to continue doing those things in addition to the strategies we will talk about over the next 6 weeks.

Before we talk about specific strategies, we want to spend some time giving you some basic information about children's emotional development. The more you understand about preschool emotional development in general, the better equipped you will be to help your child.

Emotions (which we often call "feelings" with children) are such a big part of how we experience the world. Our emotions can be positive or negative, and they can vary in how intensely we feel them. Our tendency is to want to experience positive emotions as much as possible and negative emotions as little as possible, but both positive and negative emotions are important in our lives.

Refer parents to the Emotion Development in Children handout.

Emotional Competence

Explain that emotional competence involves *understanding, expressing,* and *regulating* emotions. A major developmental task for preschool children is to develop the ability to do these things, and parents play an important role in teaching these skills. Describe each of the following aspects of emotional competence:

Emotion Knowledge or Understanding

- Identify one's own emotions

- Identify other people's emotion expression

- Predict what emotions people are likely to experience in certain situations

Emotion Expression

- Verbally and nonverbally communicate one's emotions

- Children are born being able to express emotions. Becoming emotionally competent involves learning to express emotions in ways that are adaptive (that help them get their needs met and that do not hurt others).

Emotion Regulation

- Manage or change one's emotions and expression of emotions

- Emotional knowledge and emotion expression are thought to play an important role in emotion regulation.

Discussion: How Do Emotions Help Us?

To open up discussion, ask:

What are some ways in which both positive and negative emotions can help us?

Group leaders can suggest the following if they are not raised by the group:

- Fear helps people avoid potentially dangerous situations. For example:

  - *Traffic, heights, fire*

- Anger can energize people to protect themselves against attacks. For example:

  - *Child is hit, or another child snatches her toy*

- Sadness can motivate others to meet people's needs. For example:

  - *Child gets hurt and cries; adults attend to wounds*

- Joy can help people connect with others. For example:

  - *Sharing joyful events together like holidays, weddings, and births*

Brain Development and Emotion

Refer parents to the Brain Development and Emotion handout. Inform parents that the part of the brain that is strongly associated with emotion is called the *amygdala* and is already mature at birth. Right from birth, infants can experience basic emotions, which become more complex as they develop.

Cognitive Abilities that Help Regulate Emotion

Explain that although the amygdala is responsible for experiencing emotions, other parts of the brain are important for helping to regulate and control these emotions.

Executive Function

The prefrontal cortex is like the control tower of the brain and is responsible for executive function. Among other things, executive function helps to plan responses and to control urges or initial responses to situations. For example:

■ *Samantha sees Ally playing with a toy that Samantha wants. Samantha's initial response to the situation might be to grab the toy. She has to use executive function to control that urge and use other, more socially appropriate ways of getting what she wants.*

Executive function can also help to control emotional responses.

Language

Language is often used to help regulate emotion. Adults can use language to say things that will calm down children, or, as children develop, they can use internal speech to regulate emotion.

Other Cognitive Abilities

Other cognitive abilities, such as reasoning, can also play a role in regulating emotions. For example:

■ *A child who is afraid of thunder might use reasoning (and language) to reassure herself that thunder cannot harm her.*

Note that whereas the amygdala is mature at birth, other cognitive abilities responsible for regulating emotion—particularly executive function—develop later. Thus, children have a well-developed ability to experience emotion and a less well-developed ability to regulate emotion. One of the tasks for preschoolers is to develop connections between emotion systems and these other systems.

Respecting Your Child's Emotional Experiences

Refer parents again to the Emotion Development in Children handout.

Individual Variations in Emotional Experiences

Encourage parents to recognize that people vary in how they experience emotions. This is true of both children and adults. We can vary in the following ways:

- Which emotions we feel in a given situation

- How intensely we feel the emotion

- How we express our emotions

Parents who have multiple children often know this firsthand. Remind parents that just because they would react differently to a certain situation does not mean that their children's reactions are wrong or invalid. Emphasize that they do not have to understand why a child feels an emotion to respect her emotional experience.

Discussion: Understanding Children's Perspectives

To open up discussion, ask the following:

- *Can you describe a situation in which your child was experiencing an emotion that you had a hard time understanding? How might you be able to put yourself in your child's shoes?*

- *Can you think of a time when someone did not seem to understand why you were angry about something? How did you react?*

Unconscious and Irrational Thoughts

Explain that people do not always know the reason why they feel certain emotions and discuss the following issues.

- Children may experience an emotion through conscious thoughts. If a child becomes mad, sad, or happy, she might be able to say, for example:

  - *"I feel mad because Billy took my toy."*

  - *"I feel sad because Grandma left."*

  - *"I feel happy because I won the game."*

- There are times when one's emotions occur through a nonconscious process. A child may not know what led to her feeling a certain emotion.

- Children may also express one emotion, but it is driven by another emotion. For instance, a child may express anger, but it is driven by feeling hurt.

- Emotions are often not rational, especially for children. Just because emotion is not rational does not make it any less real and does not make it wrong. Believing that one is wrong for feeling a certain way can often make one feel worse.

Hyperactive Preschoolers and Emotion Regulation

Explain that the prefrontal cortex, which is so important for controlling emotions, is not well developed in preschoolers and it is also not well developed in hyperactive children. The following script may be used:

When you have a child who is both a preschooler and hyperactive, it is a double whammy in terms of emotion regulation. We think that one reason that hyperactive preschoolers have difficulty controlling their behavior is the same reason that they have difficulty controlling their emotions—the "control tower" part of their brain is not fully developed.

However, just because there is a biological reason why hyperactive preschoolers have difficulty with emotion regulation, it does not mean that we just have to step back and wait for their brains to develop. Children's environment can shape their brain development.

Values, Beliefs, and Goals About Emotion Expression

Highlight the importance of parents' values, beliefs, and goals about emotion. The following script may be used:

People tend to have strong beliefs about emotion and emotion expression, particularly when it comes to negative emotions. As we go through life, we get a lot of messages about emotion expression. This is especially true during childhood when we tend to express emotions more. To help our children with their emotional development, we need to identify our own beliefs and assumptions about emotion and consider what messages we want to send our children about emotion.

Have parents complete the Emotion Beliefs, Values, and Goals handout and discuss.

To end this discussion, the following script may be used:

This program's goal is to teach children to express emotions in healthy and appropriate ways. We do not want to teach children to bury their feelings, but we do want them to learn to have some control over how they are expressed. To accomplish this we need to strike a balance between letting children know that it is okay to feel the way they feel, while also teaching them how to calm down and express feelings appropriately. Teaching children to bury their feelings or teaching them that their feelings are wrong will actually make it more difficult for them to control their feelings.

Important Factors that Foster Emotion Regulation

Review the following factors, which are thought to foster emotional development and competence.

Children's Play

Both pretend and physical play are related to higher emotion regulation skills and emotional understanding and expressiveness in children. Play really is preschoolers' "work."

Parenting

These are the areas that the next five sessions will emphasize:

Labeling

- Parents label their own and others' emotions. For example:

  - *"He was feeling angry, wasn't he?"*

Modeling

- Parents model healthy expression of emotions. For example:

  - *"I feel really angry right now, but I am going to try to not yell."*

- Parents also model how to regulate one's own emotions. For example:

  - *"I feel really upset right now. I need to take a deep breath to calm down."*

Coaching

Parents respond calmly and supportively when children express emotions—they act as "coaches" rather than "dismissers" of emotion. As coaches, they:

- Empathize with and validate children's emotions

- Are aware of and discuss emotions with their children

- View children's display of emotion as a time for teaching

Homework

- Have parents use the Emotions Log to track their own reactions to their children's emotions this week.

CHAPTER 12

Session 10: Teaching Children to Identify and Label Emotions

Session 10 Notes to Group Leaders

Overview

The primary goal of session 10 is to teach parents skills that focus on improving one of the key components of emotional competence: emotion knowledge/understanding. In particular, this session seeks to foster children's emotion knowledge/understanding by teaching parents to label children's, parents', and others' emotions, and to encourage children to label emotions. This session also helps parents to teach children appropriate ways of expressing their emotions.

Emotional Understanding

Although preschoolers innately experience and express emotions, they must acquire the ability to identify, label, and understand emotions. Preschool children's rapidly developing language skills can be an important vehicle for helping them better understand emotions. Parents are thought to play an important role in children's development of emotional understanding by teaching children to label emotions (Brownell, Svetlova, Anderson, Nichols, & Drummond, 2013). Parents can serve as "emotional coaches" whereby they develop the awareness of children's emotions, use emotions as teachable moments, provide validation and acceptance for children's emotions, and aid in labeling children's emotions (Denham et al., 2008). Parents who have an awareness of and discuss emotions with their children (Garner, 2006), and highlight their own and others' feelings as well as their children's responsibility for them (Denham, Mitchell-Copeland, Strandberg, Auerbach, & Blair, 1997), contribute to their children's development of emotional understanding. Parents have many rich opportunities to identify and label emotions in their children's lives, including the feelings of characters in books, on television series, or in movies. Moreover, helping parents view preschoolers' frequent emotional outbursts as opportunities for teaching children about emotions can not only foster children's emotion understanding but may also serve to shift negative attitudes that parents may have toward their children's emotions.

Effectively Expressing Emotion

The sessions also focus on helping parents teach children appropriate ways of expressing their emotions. Although children are born with the ability to express emotion, they must be socialized to express emotions in ways that are adaptive. There is a good deal of evidence that children can be successfully taught effective ways of expressing emotions through programs led by health professionals and teachers (Denham & Burton, 1996; Domitrovich, Cortes, & Greenberg, 2007; Frey, Hirschstein, & Guzzo, 2000; Webster-Stratton, Reid, & Hammond, 2001). For example, many early intervention programs designed to teach children how to experience, express, and recognize emotions have been shown to reduce children's negative emotion (Domitrovich et al., 2007) and decrease physical aggression and hostile and aggressive comments (Frey et al., 2000; Webster-Stratton et al., 2001). Teaching parents these methods for helping children express emotions appropriately may be even more effective because there are so many opportunities for parents to teach children in the moment.

Session 10 Curriculum

Materials Needed

- Teaching Children to Identify and Label Emotions handout

- Teaching Children to Identify and Label Emotions worksheet

- Teaching Children Good Ways of Expressing Emotions handout

- How Can I Show My Feelings? chart

- Labeling Feelings Log

Outline

- Review homework from last session

- Introduce the concept of emotion knowledge

- Teach parents about labeling their children's emotions

- Teach parents about labeling their own emotions

- Teach parents about labeling emotions of others

- Instruct parents on teaching children appropriate ways of expressing their emotions

- Assign homework

Homework Review

Review parents' completed Emotion Logs (approximately 10 minutes). Discuss parents' reactions to their children's emotions in the past week.

Introduction to Emotion Knowledge

Introduce the topic of emotion knowledge using the following suggested script:

Emotion knowledge means being able to identify your own emotions and other people's emotions and helps you control your own emotions. Young children who have high levels of emotion knowledge have been shown to have fewer emotional problems later in development than children who are less knowledgeable about emotion. The preschool years are a time of incredible growth in emotion knowledge, and parents can play a key role in this growth. By linking preschool children's growing language development with their already well-developed ability to feel emotions, children can begin to use language to gain control of their emotional experience.

Note that this session focuses on ways of helping children develop their knowledge about emotion using the following techniques:

- Labeling children's emotions

- Parents labeling their own emotions

- Labeling emotions of others

- Encouraging children to label others' emotions

Refer parents to the Teaching Children to Identify and Label Emotions handout throughout this session.

Labeling Children's Emotions

Tell parents that because preschool children, particularly hyperactive preschool children, have not yet mastered the ability to regulate their emotions, there is plenty of opportunity to find their children expressing both positive and negative emotions. Parents can use these moments to label their children's emotions. Note that there are many ways of labeling children's emotion, and parents should experiment with a method that is comfortable for them.

Why Label Emotions?

Discuss purposes of labeling emotions:

- It helps to link children's growing language skills to their emotional experiences.

- It helps to validate children's emotions (by recognizing and labeling the emotions they are experiencing). This can help foster the development of emotion-regulation skills over time.

Labeling Suggestions

Give the following tips for labeling children's emotions:

- Try to avoid sounding judgmental or critical. The tone should be respectful, even if one is not feeling particularly understanding.

- After labeling the emotion, try not to say anything else for a moment (e.g., count to 5 silently) to let the label sink in.

Children's Reactions

Note that if parents have not tried labeling emotions before, they may be surprised at their children's reaction. Different children respond differently but here are some typical reactions:

- Sometimes children seem to have no reaction. This does not necessarily mean that they did not hear the parent, and it is likely that the labeling had a much bigger impact than it appears.

- Sometimes children correct or deny the label. "No mom/dad, I am not mad!" If a child does this, it is best to just listen and not argue.

- Sometimes children intensify the expression of the emotion, and if it is a negative emotion, this may make parents hesitant to keep using this technique. However most children, after a moment of being more upset, will actually calm down faster than they would have if the emotion had not been labeled.

- If it is a negative emotion, it is not uncommon for a child to respond immediately by calming down.

- Sometimes children get angry (or angrier) and yell at their parents.

In-Session Exercise: Teaching Children to Identify and Label Emotions

Have parents complete the Teaching Children to Identify and Label Emotions worksheet and give feedback on their ideas. Following are suggestions for what one might say in these situations. Note that the focus here is only on labeling the feelings. Let parents know that labeling does not replace limit setting and that in a few sessions the group will discuss ways of combining labeling and limit setting.

Examples of Ways to Label Emotion

- *A child throws a puzzle piece across the room: "You seem very frustrated."*

- *A child finishes a puzzle and looks pleased: "You must be so proud!"*

- *A child's parent tells him that he can't have another cookie and he throws himself on the floor screaming: "Wow, you are really mad that you can't have another cookie!"*

- *A child is having a tantrum and it is not clear why: "Are you feeling sad or mad or both?" (this begins the important process of starting to teach children that they can experience two feelings at the same time) or "I can see how upset you are."*

- *A child runs into his parents' room during a thunderstorm and climbs in bed with them: "Did the thunder scare you?"*

- *A child takes a toy away from another child who starts crying: "Wow, look how sad that made Michael."*

- *A parent tells a child that he needs to turn off the TV and he starts whining: "I can see that you are disappointed because you love watching TV so much."*

- *A friend comes to visit and a child starts bouncing off the walls: "You are really excited about your friend coming over!"*

- *A child falls down and starts crying, but he does not really seem to be hurt: "Falling down was scary, wasn't it?"*

Labeling Your Own Emotions

Inform parents that talking about their own emotions in front of their children is a great way to model emotion expression and increase their children's emotion knowledge. In some cases, it may also be helpful for parents to follow their emotional labeling with an example of how they are coping with the emotion. For example:

- *"I am feeling very angry right now. I am going to take a few minutes and go calm down."*

- *"That makes me so happy."*

- *"I am getting frustrated about how long this is taking."*

- *"I am a little nervous about something I have to do at work today. I know it will be okay, but I still feel a little nervous."*

Labeling Tips

Encourage parents to think about the following issues when labeling their own emotions using the suggested scripts:

- *It is important to strike a balance between letting children know that you experience emotions without going overboard. You do not want to burden your child with feeling responsible for your emotional well-being.*

- *Watch your child for his reaction to your emotion expression. If you think that your child is doing something to try to get a reaction out of you, it is best not to express your emotions at that time.*

Labeling Emotions of Others

Let the group know that labeling emotions of characters in books, on TV, and other people in children's lives can be a good opportunity for teaching children about emotion when they are not preoccupied by their own emotions. For example:

- *"Wow, look how angry she is!"*

- *"It looks like that hurt his feelings."*

- *"Boy, she was really surprised!"*

- *"It looks like Raul is very sad that he is not getting a turn."*

Labeling the emotions of others is also an important part of teaching children empathy, which is critical for developing positive relationships with other people.

Teaching Children to Label

Ask parents to start the teaching process with the following.

- Encourage their children to label others' emotions. For example:

    - *"How do you think he is feeling?"*

- When their children cause someone to feel a certain way, parents can point out how the child's behavior made the other person feel, in a nonjudgmental way. For example:

    - *"Look how sad her face looked when you said that to her,"* or *"When you shared your toy with her that made her so happy!"*

Labeling Tips

Encourage parents to think about the following issues when teaching children to label others' emotions using the suggested scripts:

- *Preschoolers are just beginning to develop empathy—the ability to think about how others are feeling. This is a skill that you are starting to teach them, but you should not expect them to be able to do this easily.*

- *Even if preschoolers have empathy for someone else, it is perfectly normal for them to put their own wants and needs above others. This is especially true for hyperactive preschoolers who have difficulty controlling their desires. Part of your job is to help your children develop empathy and help them learn to balance their own needs with those of others. (But this is a process that will continue throughout childhood.)*

In-Session Exercise: Role-Play

Have parents take turns labeling their own emotions and labeling the other person's (pretending to be the child) emotions in one or two scenarios.

Come up with scenarios with the group, or suggest some. For example:

■ *You told your child that he can't go to the park today because it is raining, and he starts to cry.*

■ *You come home from work in a bad mood and find yourself taking it out on your family.*

Teaching Children Appropriate Ways of Expressing Their Emotions

Explain that emotion expression comes naturally to most children, but their natural ways of expressing emotion—particularly in the case of negative emotion—may not be appropriate and may cause problems in their interactions with others. Children are not born knowing how to express emotions in appropriate ways—parents need to teach them.

Teaching and modeling labeling of emotions is an important first step in teaching good ways of expressing emotions. Review the following methods, referring parents to the Teaching Children Good Ways of Expressing Emotions handout.

Suggest Alternatives

■ Parents can teach their children ways of expressing emotions by suggesting good alternatives when they are expressing emotion in an inappropriate way.

   ■ *"I can see that you are very angry. You may not call me names when you are angry, but you can say, 'You are making me so mad!!'"*

■ When children do express emotions in appropriate ways, parents should praise them!

Brainstorm Alternatives

■ Parents can also teach children ways of expressing emotions by brainstorming good alternatives when they are not in the heat of the moment.

■ *"I noticed that when you get really angry, you start throwing things. Let's think of things that you can do instead when you are really mad."*

Verbal versus Physical Expression

■ Parents eventually want to teach children to express their anger through words rather than physical force. But for a child who is expressing emotion physically, it may be helpful to suggest physical expressions of emotion that are safe and nondestructive, like stomping feet or punching a pillow. Parents can first teach children less negative ways of physically expressing emotions and then gradually help children shift toward ways of expressing emotions with words.

■ If a child is not already using physical expressions of emotions, parents should not encourage him to do so. There is not evidence that encouraging children to "get out their aggressions" will help them feel less angry.

Be Patient

■ When parents suggest other ways of expressing emotion while children are in the middle of feeling upset, it is unlikely that they will take these suggestions *then*. It is the next time that children might choose the suggested strategy.

In-Session Exercise: Teaching Children Good Ways of Expressing Emotions

Use the space on the Teaching Children Good Ways of Expressing Emotions handout to brainstorm good alternative ways that children can express emotions. Encourage parents to draw pictures for their children demonstrating good ways of expressing feelings.

Homework

✎ Have parents sit down with their children and fill out the How Can I Show My Feelings? chart to identify good ways their children can express emotion. Note that it may be helpful to draw pictures to go with the words they write.

✎ Have parents practice labeling their children's emotions and fill out the Labeling Feelings Log to keep track of their efforts. Remind parents to pause after labeling emotions and not jump in to correcting or criticizing.

CHAPTER 13

Sessions 11 and 12 Notes to Group Leaders

Overview

Because preschool children's ability to regulate their emotions is still in development, emotional meltdowns are commonplace (Wakschlag et al., 2012). Hyperactive preschoolers are even more likely than typically developing preschoolers to express frequent negative emotion (Harvey, Friedman-Weieneth, Goldstein, & Sherman, 2007). The way in which parents respond to their children's negative emotion is thought to be one important component of emotion socialization. For example, providing support and assistance when children are upset (i.e., "coaching") contributes to children's emotional well-being, whereas dismissing and minimizing children's negative emotion tends to be associated with poorer emotional competence in children (Denham et al., 2008).

Validating Children's Emotions

One of the key goals of sessions 11 and 12 is to help parents learn to validate rather than invalidate their children's emotions. This is an important part of effective emotion socialization; children who experience invalidating childhood environments are at risk for developing a variety of emotional and personality difficulties (e.g., Robertson, Kimbrel, & Nelson-Gray, 2013). However, validating negative emotions can be very difficult for parents to do. Children's negative emotions can elicit strong physiological and emotional reactions from parents (Frodi & Lamb, 1980), which may naturally lead parents to invalidate their children's negative emotions in an effort to reduce them. However, parents' attempts to squelch negative emotions in their children may have the opposite effect. Invalidating responses to negative emotion, in fact, lead to greater negative emotion and arousal than validating responses (Shenk & Fruzzetti, 2011).

Common Misconceptions

In some cases, parents' resistance to validating children's emotions stems from misunderstandings about what validating means, so it is important to address these common misconceptions. First, validating does not require parents to engage in long discussions about the negative emotion. Short, simple validations, or supportive silence can be highly effective. In fact, it is not uncommon for some parents to go overboard in their validations, and parents should be cautioned against overdoing it. Second, validating a child's emotion does not necessarily mean condoning any misbehavior or inappropriate expression of emotion that may be coinciding with the emotion. Helping parents separate the child's emotions (which are normal) from their behavior (which may be undesirable) is essential. Parents' resistance to validating children's emotions can also come from an inability to see the logic in a child's emotional reactions. Remind parents that preschoolers can be remarkably illogical, and that the goal is not to agree with the child or to understand why the child is feeling the way she is feeling, but to simply acknowledge the child's feelings without judgment. Even for parents who fully accept the notion of validating their children's feelings, validating can be very difficult. Children's negative emotions often occur in the context of parent–child conflict, and parents' own emotional reactions often make it difficult to validate. Acknowledge the challenges of validating children's emotions, and emphasize that parents' goal is to engage in more coaching and less dismissing, but they need not be perfect to be effective.

Session 11 Curriculum

Materials Needed

- Validating Negative Emotion handout

- Helping Your Child Calm Down handout

- Validating Emotions and Helping Your Child Calm Down Log

Outline

- Review homework from last session

- Introduce topic of handling children's negative emotions

- Teach parents how to validate their children's emotions

- Teach parents how to help their children to calm down

- Assign homework

Homework Review

Review homework from last session (approximately 10 minutes), including the completed How Can I Show My Feelings? chart and the Labeling Feelings Log. Discuss any difficulties parents had with labeling emotions.

Introduction to Handling Children's Negative Emotion

Introduce handling negative emotion using the following suggested script:

During the next two sessions we will be focusing on how to handle children's emotional outbursts. One of the hardest but most important parts of parenting is knowing what to do when your child is upset, so we want to spend extra time on this issue.

Highlight the following points.

Parents are Wired to Respond to Children's Negative Emotion

Explain that parents are wired to respond to children's negative emotions and that this is helpful during infancy, because it is an important way of making sure that parents give infants the attention they need. However, children's negative emotions have also been shown to increase adults' stress, which can sometimes make parents do things that they do not mean to do or do things that can interfere with children's emotional development in the long term.

Most Parents' First Instinct Is to Make a Negative Emotion Go Away

For discussion, ask the group:

What are some things parents sometimes say to try to make their children's negative feelings stop?

Here are examples:

- *"Don't be sad."*

- *"There is nothing to be afraid of."*

- *"There is no reason to be upset."*

- *"Pull yourself together."*

- *"Stop crying."*

Parents Can Rarely Change Children's Feelings by Telling Them to Stop Feeling a Certain Way

Telling children to stop feeling the way they do often makes children hold onto those feelings or express the feelings even longer. Highlight the following:

- There are things parents can do or say to help their children feel better, but telling a child to feel differently is not usually effective.

- It can be very difficult to resist the urge to tell children not to feel sad or angry! It tends to be something that people do instinctively both with children and with other adults.

Remember to Consider Prevention

- Remind parents of the preventative strategies discussed earlier. Preventing a meltdown is much easier than handling a meltdown! Of course parents cannot protect children from ever being upset (nor should they), but warding off some of the emotionally difficult situations can be helpful.

There is Not One Right Way to Handle Children's Negative Emotions

Emphasize that the best response depends on the situation, the individual child, and the parent's own thoughts and feelings.

Validating Emotions

Tell the group that validating emotions means acknowledging and accepting feelings. Explain that one of the most important things to do when children are experiencing emotion—both positive and negative emotion—is to validate their feelings. This is particularly important and difficult to do when children are experiencing negative feelings. Much of the discussion will focus on validating negative emotions in children.

Explain that when people invalidate another person's feelings, it tends to make those feelings more intense. One of the best ways of moving on is to accept the feelings, even if they are not rational. Parents can help children do this by accepting their children's feelings as normal, even if parents do not think they would feel the same way.

During this section, refer parents to the Validating Negative Emotion handout.

How to Validate Feelings

Note that there are many things parents can do to validate feelings, both through their words and their actions:

Do

- Label emotions (as discussed last session). For example:

  - *"I can see how angry you are."*

- Express understanding. For example:

  - *"I can understand how disappointed you are to not have a cookie."*

- Directly tell the child that it is okay to feel the way she is feeling. For example:

  - *"It is okay to feel sad/mad/frustrated."*

- Simply be with the child quietly while she is experiencing negative feelings. This can be amazingly powerful and helpful. This is an especially good tool to use if a parent is not feeling empathic toward the child and finds it difficult to be genuine in verbally validating the child.

- Let the child know that negative emotions feel very strong while a person is experiencing them, but they do pass with time. For example:

  - *"I know that you are feeling so upset right now. When I feel really upset, I find that if I just let myself feel upset, the feelings start to get smaller by themselves after a little while."*

Don't

- Don't hurry to fix children's negative emotions.

- Don't tell children to stop feeling the way they are feeling.

Clarifying Misconceptions

- Parents do not have to agree with their children to validate their feelings.

- Parents can validate children's feelings without validating the way children are expressing their feelings if they are expressing their feelings in hurtful or destructive ways.

- Validating children's feelings does not mean giving in to children. Parents can express understanding about why their children are upset while at the same time setting a limit. For example:

  - *"I can understand how disappointed you are to not have a cookie. (Wait 5 seconds.) You still can't have a cookie before dinner because it's not good for you."*

Effective Validation is Genuine

Explain to parents that their validation will be more effective if it can be genuine. The following script may be used:

Validation is best when it's genuine. This means trying your best to understand what your child is feeling. To do this you need to try to put yourself in your child's shoes, not as a rational adult but imagining yourself as a preschooler. This can be very difficult, but it is important not only for helping you to genuinely validate but also because you will be modeling and teaching your child how to take another person's perspective.

Discussion: Understanding a Child's Perspective

For group discussion, pose the following:

Think of a situation when your child was upset and you found it hard to empathize. Now try to imagine yourself as a preschool child in that situation having that same reaction (not as an adult in that situation!). Can you understand the situation from your child's shoes? How would you want to be treated?

Feelings versus Misbehavior

Parents often have a hard time validating a child's feelings because they see the child's outburst as misbehavior or as a sign that the child is spoiled. Make the following points:

- Emotional outbursts that come from genuine emotion are not misbehavior—disobeying, being destructive, or being aggressive is misbehavior—feeling sad or angry is not misbehavior.

- It is true that children who always get their way are likely to get upset when they are denied something. The best way to avoid spoiling a child is to set clear limits and to not let a child always have her way. When a child does get upset because she does not get her own way, invalidating her feeling is not going to help her be less spoiled.

Validating in Moderation

Sometimes when parents first try validating their children's feelings, they tend to go overboard. Highlight the following:

- Often, less is more when it comes to validation. One simple statement can be enough.

- Sometimes silence can be the best way for parents to communicate to a child that they see her emotions as a normal part of life.

In-Session Exercise: Role-Play

Have parents break up into groups of 2 or 3 and practice validating, using the following scenarios:

- *Child asks for a cookie before dinner. Parent says no, and child begins to wail.*

- *Child falls down and scrapes her knee and begins to cry.*

Helping Children to Calm Down

Explain that strong feelings are often like a storm, with periods of high intensity followed by periods of lower intensity. It is difficult to sustain strong feelings for long periods of time, so in most cases they will pass on their own. However, children can vary in how long they typically experience bouts of intense feelings.

To open up discussion, ask parents the following:

- *What is your child's typical pattern of experiencing negative emotions?*

- *How long do they usually last? Does the intensity go up and down?*

To end the discussion, the following script may be used:

Being aware of your child's typical pattern can help you cope better with outbursts. It often feels like the outbursts will go on forever, so reminding yourself of the typical length of the outburst may help you get through it more easily.

Techniques for Calming Down

Note that some techniques are better for the more intense phases of emotion and some techniques are better for less intense phases. Giving a child space is typically best during the more intense periods, while other techniques are better used when the intensity comes down a notch.

Review with parents the following techniques for helping calm a child down after having validated the child's feelings (refer parents to the Helping Your Child Calm Down handout).

Give Children Some Time and/or Space to Calm Down

- Walk away.

- Be with the child physically, and either say nothing or validate the child's feelings.

- Sometimes children need to be left alone, and sometimes children need company when they are feeling negative emotions. Parents can figure this out by trial and error or by asking a child if she wants to be left alone. When making this decision, parents also need to pay attention to their own needs. If a parent thinks the child wants company but the parent needs some time and space, it may be best to leave the room.

When Giving Time and/or Space Is Not an Option

- In some cases children get really upset and need time to calm down, but parents do not have the luxury of giving them time to calm down. For example:

  - *Just before leaving for work/preschool*

  - *In public*

  - *When it is time to go to bed*

- It is fine for parents to move their children while they are upset (e.g., put them in the car, move them to a location where the screaming will not disturb others, put them in bed). Parents just need to be careful not to hurt children while moving them—children are likely to be thrashing, and parents may not be feeling very calm themselves.

- Parents should not try to have a conversation with their children until both parents and children have calmed down.

Using Distraction

Distraction can be useful in helping negative feelings pass more quickly, but note:

- Parents should be careful not to jump into distraction too quickly.

- It may be helpful to simply let children be upset for 5 minutes, and, if they have not calmed down on their own, parents can try distraction.

- Parents should be careful that they are not rewarding their children's tantrums by giving them something special whenever they are upset.

- Distracting with activities is generally better than distracting with treats.

Other Techniques

- Parents can suggest that their children take deep breaths (and breathe with them!).

- Parents can encourage children to count to 10 or can count out loud for their children.

- Parents can sing to their children.

Things to Think About

Other pointers to give parents include:

- Parents need to recognize their own reactions to their children's negative emotions. If children are making their parents feel upset, it is fine for parents to take a break and leave the room.

- If there are situations that parents anticipate will make their children upset, it may be helpful to talk through with their children ways to help prepare them. For example:

  - *Whenever your child has a play date, she gets upset when the other child plays with her toys. Talk with your child ahead of time about choosing certain special toys that she does not want the other child to play with, and put those toys away before the play date.*

In-Session Exercise: Role-Play

Have parents break up into groups of 2 or 3 and practice validating and helping the child to calm down, using the following scenarios:

- *Child wants to watch a video and the parent says no. The child bursts into tears.*

- *Child throws herself on the floor in a tantrum for no apparent reason.*

Homework

- Have parents work on validating their children's feelings and helping their children calm down, describing how they handled situations on the Validating Emotions and Helping Your Child Calm Down Log.

Session 12 Curriculum

Materials Needed

- What Do I Do When My Child is Upset? handout

- Example 1 handout

- Example 2 handout

- Helping Children Change Thoughts handout

- What Can I Do When My Child is Upset? worksheet

- Anxiety in Preschool Children handout

- Handling Your Child's Negative Emotions Log

Outline

- Review homework from last session

- Teach parents steps for handling children's negative emotions

- Discuss ways to help children overcome anxiety and fear

- Assign homework

Homework Review

Review homework from last session (approximately 10–15 minutes), checking parents' completed Validating Emotions and Helping Your Child to Calm Down logs and discussing any difficulties they had handling situations.

Handling Children's Negative Emotion

Introduce this session using the following suggested script:

Last week we talked about validating emotions and helping children to calm down. Today we will expand on those ideas, talking about what to do when your child is not only experiencing negative emotion but is also misbehaving.

We are providing a flowchart that may be helpful as a starting place in guiding you when your child is upset. Remember that it is just a guide; you will need to use your own judgment in adjusting it to particular situations.

Refer parents to the What Do I Do When My Child is Upset? worksheet. *Note:* This flowchart is designed particularly for dealing with anger, frustration, and sadness. Tell parents that the group will later discuss how this might be modified when children are feeling anxiety.

Step 1: Validate

Refer to earlier discussions of labeling emotion and expressing understanding.

Step 2: Handle Misbehavior

Note that misbehavior may also be occurring with the negative feelings.

- Once parents have validated their children's feelings, if children are also misbehaving (being aggressive, destructive, or not listening), parents should handle the misbehavior using the techniques discussed earlier (e.g., using commands, consequences, time out).

- When parents are handling misbehavior, it is important to make a distinction between feelings and behavior. For example:

  - *"It is okay to feel mad, but you may not hit other people/throw things, even when you are feeling mad."*

- In some cases it may make sense to skip to step 3 before handling the misbehavior.

Step 3: Give Children Time to Calm Down

Refer to earlier discussions of giving children time and/or space to calm down.

In-Session Exercise: Role-Play

Have parents break into pairs and role-play the following scenario:

Your child misbehaved earlier in the day and you took away his dessert. After dinner your child begins to tantrum because you did not let him have dessert, and he comes up to you and starts hitting you.

Step 4 for Handling Negative Emotion

Once children are calm enough to have a conversation, parents can consider what caused their children to be upset and whether it makes sense to problem solve with their children or help their children think differently about the problem to make the situation less upsetting.

Note that parents do not need to engage in step 4 every time their children get upset about something. In many cases it is best to validate, handle the misbehavior, and then move on. Advise parents to use step 4 when they have the time and patience for it and not to overuse it—they will not want to have a long conversation with their children every time they are upset.

Problem Solving

- If parents think there is a solution to the problem, they should engage in problem solving.

- If parents think that the problem cannot be solved, they should explain why. For example:

  - *"I know that you are really disappointed that you can't watch another TV show. But it is not good for people to watch too much TV."*

Changing Thinking

Parents can help their children change how they think about the event, as the way we think about a situation can often affect how we feel about it.

- When parents are doing this, it is important not to discount the negative aspects of an event. Children will likely react by trying even harder to convince parents why things are so awful.

- Parents should make sure to validate (i.e., express understanding, label emotion), and let children have time to feel their support, then work on helping their children to think differently about the situation.

Example of Handling Negative Emotion

Refer parents to the Helping Children Change Thoughts handout. Review the example: *Your child comes home from school and is sad because two other children did not want him to play with them.*

1. First validate.

   - *"That must have really hurt your feelings. Nobody likes to feel left out." Allow your child to respond to what you have said. (If possible, being close to your child—e.g., holding your child on your lap during this conversation—can be helpful.)*

2. Next, problem-solve.

   "I wonder if we can come up with some ideas about how to solve this problem if it happens again."

3. Or, help children change how they think about events.

   - Focus on other positive events. For example:

- *"That was a sad thing that happened in your day. Were there happy things that happened to you today?"*

- Help children put themselves in another person's shoes. For example:

  - *"I know that sometimes you are not in the mood to play with some of your friends, even when you really like those friends, but then the next day you often want to play with them again. I wonder if they felt the same way."*

- Talk about the fact that sometimes people get their way, and sometimes they do not. For example:

  - *Your child is upset about having to turn off the TV. "Sometimes we get to do things our way and sometimes we do not. It would be nice if we could always do things our way, but I am afraid that life is not like that."*

- Help children in accepting imperfection. It is common for preschoolers to get upset when their visions are ahead of their abilities. It is a slow process, but parents can begin to help them understand that things do not have to be perfect to be wonderful. For example:

  - *"I can see how frustrated you are that your castle is not coming out the way you want it to. (Pause, comfort, give space.) I know that you want it to come out just right, but a lot of times we just have to say, 'Oh well! Good enough!'"*

In-Session Exercise: Examples of Handling Negative Emotion

Have parents read through the Session 12 Examples 1 and 2 handouts. Parents can role-play the different parts. These vignettes provide examples of how to problem-solve and how to help children think differently about events. Emphasize to parents that they would not necessarily engage in these Step 4 activities every time their children get upset.

In-Session Exercise: What Can I Do When My Child Is Upset?

Help parents plan their strategy for handling their children's negative emotions by having them complete and discuss the What Can I Do When My Child is Upset? worksheet.

Helping Children Overcome Anxiety and Fear

Inform parents that fears are extremely common among preschoolers, and there are some important things to keep in mind when their children are upset out of anxiety or fear (refer to the Anxiety in Preschool Children handout).

Most Children Outgrow Their Fears Naturally

- Unless a child's anxiety is causing big problems, it is often fine to let the child outgrow fears.

- If a child's anxiety is causing big problems, it is good to get help from a mental health professional to help address the child's anxiety.

Facing Fears

- Helping children to face their fears can help them overcome anxiety, and avoiding fears can make them worse. But it is also important to be careful not to push them too hard, or it can make things worse.

- It is important to walk a fine line between gently encouraging children to face their fears without pushing them if they are not ready.

- Sometimes it is useful to help children gradually face their fears. For example, if a child is afraid of big dogs, try to first arrange for him to play with smaller dogs in safe situations; then have the child be as close to a friendly but large dog as he can comfortably be, and then gradually have the child get used to being closer and closer to the large dog.

Other Tips for Helping Children with Anxiety and Fear

- It may be helpful to combine validation with reassurance. For example:

  - *"Thunder sounds really scary to you, doesn't it? Even though it sounds scary, it cannot hurt you."*

- Parents should avoid shaming their children, calling them a baby, or telling them to be a big boy or a big girl.

- When a child does successfully face his fears, parents should point out to him how his feelings changed over time. For example:

- *"You used to be really afraid of dogs, but now it seems like you are getting used to them."*

In-Session Exercise: Children's Fears

Ask parents if their children have fears that the group can discuss. Role-play how to handle these fears. If time allows, continue to troubleshoot and/or role-play handling negative emotion.

Homework

- Have parents continue to try these techniques when their children become upset, and complete the Handling Your Child's Negative Emotions Log.

CHAPTER 14

Session 13: Giving Children Opportunities to Experience Positive Emotion

Session 13 Notes to Group Leaders

Overview

Hyperactive preschoolers frequently have negative interactions with other children and adults (Barkley, 2006). Other children may get annoyed with them because they are impulsive, and parents and teachers often become frustrated with them because they do not listen and disrupt the class. These interactions may partly explain why these children are more likely to experience negative emotions. Session 13 seeks to counterbalance some of this negative emotion by helping parents to provide children with opportunities to experience positive emotion.

Parenting Techniques to Foster Positive Emotion

First, it is important for parents to help children engage in enjoyable activities that foster positive emotion. Experiencing positive emotion has important benefits in people's lives and contributes to physical, psychological, and social well-being (Lyubomirsky, King, & Diener, 2005; Shin et al., 2011). Helping parents brainstorm as a group about fun activities (including no-cost or low-cost activities) can allow parents to learn new ideas from each other.

Second, children thrive when they have opportunities to succeed. Teaching parents how to use scaffolding gives them an important tool for helping their children succeed (Hammond, Müller, Carpendale, Bibok, & Liebermann-Finestone, 2012), while also challenging their children. Scaffolding provides children with the opportunity to learn by working at the appropriate level—one that is not too easy or too challenging (Vygotsky, 1978; Wood, Bruner, & Ross, 1976). Using this approach, children can take small but challenging steps toward an eventual goal. By setting up these "successive approximations," the child has many opportunities for success along the way to the final goal.

Third, it is important for parents to emphasize their preschooler's strengths and to convey their love for their children. Because hyperactive preschoolers often engage in challenging behavior, it can be easy for parents to focus on their children's weaknesses instead of strengths and for children to worry that they are not loved. Thus, children who are likely most in need of positive feedback from their parents may be least likely to receive it.

Finally, teaching parents to help their children use positive thinking provides parents with an important tool to help children experience positive emotions even in the face of challenges. Using this technique, parents can lay the groundwork for teaching children that we can use our thoughts to change how we feel. This emotion-regulation strategy can be highly effective, and use of the strategy can contribute to children's emotional well-being (Snyder et al., 1997).

Session 13 Curriculum

Materials Needed

- Setting Children Up for Success: Scaffolding handout

- Example of Scaffolding at Home handout

- Scaffolding at Home worksheet

- Giving Children Opportunities to Experience Positive Emotion handout

- My Child's Strengths worksheet

- Emphasizing Your Child's Strengths worksheet

Outline

- Review homework

- Introduce the topic of positive emotions

- Teach parents about positive activities and scaffolding

- Discuss other ways to give children opportunities to experience positive emotion

- Assign homework

Homework Review

Review parents' completed What Can I Do When My Child is Upset? logs (approximately 10 minutes). Discuss any difficulties. Encourage parents to continue to try these techniques when their children become upset.

Introduction to Positive Emotion

Introduce the topic of positive emotions using the following suggested script:

We talked several weeks ago about the fact that children who are hyperactive get frequent negative feedback from the environment. It is important to go out of your way to balance that negative with positive. In addition to strategies we've already talked about for increasing children's positive emotion, like praise and positive attention, today we will talk about other ways of helping children experience positive feelings.

Positive Activities and Scaffolding

Review the following approaches to increasing positive affect in children.

Helping Your Child Find Fun Things to Do

Note that this does not have to cost money! Ideas:

- Going to a playground

- Playing imaginary games

- Going for a walk

- Playing hide and seek

- Hiding an object and telling the child if she is getting "warmer" (closer) or "colder" (further away)

- Setting up an obstacle course and seeing how fast a child can run through it

Scaffolding: Setting Children up for Success

Explain that scaffolds help workers to be right at the level they need to be working. The height of the scaffold can be increased when the worker completes a particular area. Parents are scaffolds for their children. The trick is figuring out the right height of the scaffold so that the child can work on the right area. If the scaffold is too low or moves too slowly, the child will not get challenged and grow to her potential. If the scaffold is too high or moves too quickly, the child will be working on areas that she is not ready for, will become frustrated, and will stop trying.

Note that moving too slowly or too quickly are both common, but most parents have a tendency to move too quickly. If in doubt, it is better to move too slowly than too quickly.

Refer parents to the Setting Children Up for Success: Scaffolding handout during this section.

In-Session Exercise: Scaffolding

Using the Scaffolding at Home worksheet, have parents think of activities that are challenging for their children. It could be getting themselves ready in the morning, helping around the house, or learning to do something new. Have them make a list of goals within this activity that are easy for their children to accomplish. Next have them make a list of goals within the activity that are a little challenging for their children, but are things their children can do. They should then make a list of goals within this activity that are very difficult for their children. The goal is to set the scaffold halfway between easy and a bit challenging.

See Figure 14.1 for the example of eating dinner together, and refer parents to the Example of Scaffolding at Home handout.

Easy	A bit challenging	Very difficult
Sitting in seat while chewing (but getting up between bites)	Sitting at the table for 3 minutes	Sitting at the table for 5 minutes
Standing (but not sitting) next the table while eating	Alternating between sitting and standing at the table for 5 minutes	Alternating between sitting and standing at the table for 10 minutes
Eating hotdogs, macaroni and cheese, grilled cheese	Eating one raw vegetable	Eating any cooked vegetable
Using manners once during the meal (e.g. saying please or thank you)	Using manners three times during the meal	Using manners throughout the meal

Figure 14.1

Types of Goals for Eating Dinner Together

1st Week

- Parents should praise children for tasks they accomplish on the easy list.

- As much as possible, parents should ignore children's inability to achieve goals on the second and third list.

- If children accomplish a goal on the second or third list, parents should make a big deal of it!

2nd Week and Beyond

- Parents should continue what they did during the first week, but slowly encourage their children to try things on the next list.

Things to Think About

Give the following pointers to parents in setting their children up for success:

- Sometimes it is helpful to put in an age comparison in praise to help it feel genuine. This is especially helpful if a child has an older sibling and can see that she is not as good as the older sibling at something. For example:

  - *"Wow, you are really good at soccer for a 4-year-old!"*

- Adjusting expectations will often mean adjusting parents' behavior. A parent may decide that a child really is not ready to be able to sit in a restaurant, so the parent may need to avoid taking her to restaurants until she is ready. Of course there may be some situations that simply cannot be changed and that will be very challenging for the child, but limiting such situations can be helpful.

What About When Children Do Not Succeed?

Let parents know that they will naturally sometimes end up in situations that are very challenging for their children. However, the more opportunities children have at home for success the easier it will be for them to face these challenging situations.

Suggest things parents can do when their children do not succeed:

- Remind the child that no one is perfect. Give specific examples of ways in which people (including parents!) are not perfect.

- Praise the child's effort: "Not quite, but good try!"

- Emphasize the difficulty of the task: "Wow that is really hard!"

Other Ways to Give Children Opportunities to Experience Positive Emotion

Refer parents to the Giving Children Opportunities to Experience Positive Emotion handout during this section.

Emphasizing Children's Strengths

- Encourage parents to take a moment every day to tell their children at least one thing they like about their children. Bedtime is a great time to do this.

- This can be very difficult to do when children are having a hard day. This needs to be genuine, so parents should not force themselves to do it if they do not think they can be genuine. But remember, parents telling children things that they like about them is not the same as excusing bad behavior. For example:

  - *"I was not very happy with how much you and your brother were fighting today, but I wanted to let you know how much I appreciate how well you usually get along."*

In-Session Exercise: My Child's Strengths

Have parents make a list of things that they like about their children on the My Child's Strengths worksheet. They should hang this list in a location where they and their children can see it every day.

Affection/Warmth/Expressing Your Love

Most parents know it is important to express love and affection, but it is difficult to remember to do. Generate a list of different ways of conveying love with the group and touch on the following points.

■ Parents should directly tell their children that they love them. Again, bedtime is often a good time for this.

■ It is important for parents to convey that their love is unconditional and to separate their disapproval of their children's behavior from their love of their children. For example:

  ■ *"Did you know that I love you even when I get mad at you?"*

  ■ *A parent–child "vow": "Did you know that I love you when you are happy or sad, when you are behaving well and when you are not, when you are good at doing something and when you have a hard time doing something? No matter what."*

  ■ *"I did not like it that you were not listening to me tonight at bedtime, but even when I do not like what you are doing, I still love you."*

■ Parents should convey to children that their worth is separate from their achievements.

Helping Children Look at the Bright Side

Discuss with the group that the way we view the events in our lives can have a big impact on how we feel about those events. Focusing on the positive rather than the negative aspect of events can often help us feel better about the event.

In fact, the English language has many expressions about focusing on the positive.

- Look at the bright side.

- Look at the glass as half full, rather than half empty.

- Find the silver lining in the cloud.

- When someone gives you lemons, make lemonade.

- Look at the world through rose-colored glasses.

Suggestions

Give suggestions and examples of how parents can help their children look at the bright side.

- Parents can help their children look at the bright side by modeling how they look at events in their own lives, and parents can also help their children change to thinking about events in a more positive light. For example:

  - *You get stuck in traffic: "Oh well—this gives us extra time to play a game while we wait. Do you want to play, "I spy?"*

  - *Your child accidentally spills milk: "Oops! No use crying over spilled milk. Here is a sponge so you can help me clean it up."*

  - *Your child skins her knee and cries: "Ooh, that looks like it really hurts. I am so sorry you got hurt." (Give child a chance to cry.) "Let's get that cleaned up and put a bandage on it—I bet it will feel better in no time."*

- Remind parents that if their children are upset about something, it is important to not invalidate the negative aspects of an event. Children will likely react by trying even harder to convince their parents why things are so awful. Parents should first validate (i.e., express understanding, label the emotion) and let their children have time to feel their parents' support; then parents can work on helping their children to think differently about the situation.

Homework

- ✎ Have parents try to tell their children at least one thing they like about them every day and fill out the Emphasizing Your Child's Strengths worksheet.

- ✎ Ask parents to try to convey love to their children every day.

- ✎ Have parents practice focusing on the positive rather than the negative aspect of events. Have them note how this perspective affected their and their children's experience.

CHAPTER 15

Session 14: Modeling Emotion Regulation and Expression

Session 14 Notes to Group Leaders

Overview

Session 14, the last session, focuses on helping parents model emotion regulation and emotion expression, reflects back on the tools that have been taught in this program, and provides an opportunity for troubleshooting.

Emotion Regulation

Parents contribute to the development of children's emotional regulation by modeling and regulating their own emotions (Denham et al., 2008). Thus, part of this session emphasizes ways parents can manage and regulate their own emotions to serve as models for their children. As group leaders discuss strategies that parents can use to manage their emotions, it is also important to validate and normalize parents' emotional experiences. Being a parent is not easy, particularly with a hyperactive preschooler. Parents of hyperactive children are at increased risk for experiencing stress and depression (Barkley, 2006). Often parents forget about their own well-being when they have children, particularly challenging children. However, it is important to remind parents that they are likely to be most present and most effective as parents if they take time to care for themselves. It is also important to note that although the strategies taught in this session may be helpful in managing symptoms of depression, it will be important to be prepared to provide a referral for parents who may be clinically depressed and in need of professional help in coping with their own symptoms.

Emotion Expression

The second portion of this session provides parents with strategies for healthily expressing their own emotions. Much of children's emotional learning occurs in interactions with their parents, as parents express their own emotions through verbal and nonverbal emotional communications (Halberstadt, 1991). Modeling effective ways of communicating emotion (e.g., labeling their own emotions calmly, using "I" statements), expressing well-modulated negative emotion, and verbalizing one's efforts to control expression of emotion provide children with opportunities to learn and practice regulating their own negative emotions (Denham et al., 2008).

Review and Troubleshooting

This program introduces a vast array of parenting strategies, and it can be overwhelming for parents to try to use them all. During this final session, it can be helpful to go back and review the tools parents have learned in this program and help them reflect on which tools they found to be most useful. This can also be an opportunity for continued troubleshooting, which can be done individually or in the group format. Encourage parents to continue to seek support, given the challenges of raising a hyperactive child. A booster session a few weeks after the program ends can provide parents with additional support following the completion of the program. This will give parents the opportunity to troubleshoot issues, review the tools discussed during the program, and receive support.

Session 14 Curriculum

Materials Needed

- Modeling Emotion Regulation handout

- Modeling Emotion Expression handout

- What's in a Parent's Toolbox? handout

- What Parenting Tools Work Best for You? worksheet

Outline

- Review homework from the last session

- Discuss how parents can model emotion regulation

- Discuss how parents can express their emotions in healthy ways

- Wrap up the program

Homework Review

Review homework from the last session (approximately 10 minutes), including parents' completed Emphasizing Your Child's Strengths worksheets. Discuss any difficulties in conveying love or focusing on the positive.

Modeling Emotion Regulation

Introduce modeling emotion regulation using the following suggested script:

One of the most powerful ways that children learn about emotion is through modeling—watching others around them deal with and express emotion. Children tend to be very aware of emotions in others, and even when you think they are not paying attention, they are. They will learn by watching you express emotion to them and to other family members, and by how you react to other people's emotions as well as theirs. They will take what they learn to other settings as they grow.

Today we will talk about how to use our own experiences with emotion to teach children about how to handle their emotion. We will talk about two things. First we will talk about strategies for bringing down the intensity of our feelings when we experience strong emotions. Then we will talk about good ways of expressing our emotions and using these situations as opportunities to teach our children.

Refer parents to the Modeling Emotion Regulation handout in this section.

Managing Your Own Emotions

Explain to parents that the goal is not to stop themselves from having strong emotions—having strong emotions is natural when you are a parent. The goal is for parents to figure out how to manage strong emotions when they occur.

Note that everyone finds different things helpful.

To open up group discussion, ask:

What strategies are helpful for you when you are really upset?

- Review any of the following strategies that were not brought up in discussion:

  - *Count to 10*

  - *Take slow, deep breaths*

  - *Take a break (making sure children are safe and monitored)*

  - *Exercise*

  - *Talk with someone (call a friend)*

  - *Use calming statements*

  - *Change thoughts about the situation*

- Explain that children will benefit simply from seeing their parents use these strategies, but it also may be helpful to explicitly talk to their children about their efforts to manage their emotions. For example:

  - *"I am angry right now so I am going to the other room for a few minutes to cool down."*

Taking Care of One's Own Emotional Well-Being

Discuss with parents the importance of taking care of their own emotional well-being. The following script may be used:

On airplanes we are often instructed to put on our own oxygen masks before helping our children put on theirs. This is because you need to be able to function yourself in order to help your child. The same holds true for your role as a parent. You need to take enough care of yourself that you can be present for your child. Sometimes parents feel guilty for taking time away from their children, but no matter how much we love our children, taking some time away from them to restore our energy can be important. Every parent's needs are different, so do not judge your own needs based on what others around you appear to need.

To open up group discussion, ask:

What things can you do to help decrease stress?

Expressing Emotions in Healthy Ways

Refer parents to the Modeling Emotion Expression handout. Encourage parents to:

- Label their own feelings as calmly as possible.

- Tell others how they feel without lashing out at them.

- Use "I" statements. For example:

  - *"I feel frustrated when I feel like I am the only one in the house cleaning up,"* instead of, *"How many times do I have to tell you to clean up after yourself?!"*

- Avoid sarcasm, belittling, and saying mean things when they are angry.

- Simply say nothing if they are so upset that they do not think they can express themselves in a healthy way.

Parents Can Talk With Children About Their Own Efforts

Tell parents that they can also be good models by talking to their children about their own efforts to control the way they express their emotions. For example:

- *"Right now I am angry and feel like yelling, but I am going to try not to."*

Apologize

- Note that everyone says things that they do not mean, and the important thing is to apologize when it does happen. An apology cannot take away a mean comment, but it certainly helps a lot. For example:

  - *"Even though I was upset, I should not have said mean things to you. I am sorry I did that."*

- Reassure parents that everyone yells sometimes, and it is a normal part of parenting. Our goal is to try not to yell, but encourage parents not to be too hard on themselves if they do sometimes.

Letting Children See a Glimpse of Adults' Emotional World

Note that some parents try to shield their children entirely from adult emotional experiences, and some parents have difficulty with adult emotional experiences spilling over too much into children's lives.

Tell parents that the goal is to have a balance between allowing their children to see glimpses of healthy expression of adult emotional experiences without burdening them with frequent and intense adult emotions.

Crying In Front of Children

Reassure parents that crying in front of their children teaches them that crying is a normal way of expressing sadness. Highlight the following:

- It can be upsetting for children to see their parents crying frequently. If parents find themselves crying a great deal, it may be best to limit how often their children see them crying.

- It can be helpful to talk with children about parents' crying. For example:

  - *"I was really sad about our cat dying, but crying helped me get rid of some of the sadness."*

Fighting Between Parents in Front of Children

Having adults yell or be mean to each other in front of children can be very upsetting for children. Advise parents to have this type of fight behind closed doors. Highlight the following:

- It can be very good for children to see their parents work out differences in constructive ways, so parents can do this in front of their children when it is an appropriate topic.

- If children do see their parents fighting intensely, they should talk to their children about what they saw. For example:

  - *"I know you saw me fighting with your dad yesterday, and we were both really angry. After you went to bed, we talked through our problem and we are both feeling much better today. Was it upsetting for you to see us fight?"*

Wrap-Up

As this is the last session, take some time to review program tools and plan for continued support.

Parenting Tools

Note that this program has presented many different tools. Some tools work better for some families than others, and some tools that do not work now may work better in the future, so advise parents to keep them all in their toolbox (refer to the What's in A Parent's Toolbox? handout).

Ask parents to think about what tools seem to work well, and write them on the What Parenting Tools Work Best for You? worksheet as a reminder to keep using them. Also, encourage group members to think about what they want to continue working on as parents.

Use any remaining time to troubleshoot.

Continued Support

Finally, talk about the importance of continuing to get support. The following script may be used:

Parenting is challenging, and everyone needs some support, but when you have a child who is hyperactive it can be particularly important to have someone to support you and provide some guidance in helping you figure out how to best manage your child's behavior.

Additional booster sessions scheduled several weeks following this last session can be helpful for reinforcing the strategies taught in this program and helping parents troubleshoot any difficulties they may still be having.

Appendix: Parent Handouts and Worksheets

Session 1: Introduction and Managing Hyperactive Behavior

Session 2: Using Praise Effectively

Session 3: Increasing Positive Interactions and Using Attention to Shape Children's Behavior

Session 4: Setting Up an Effective Reward System

Session 5: Using Commands to Guide Children's Behavior

Session 6: Using Logical and Natural Consequences and Rewards

Session 7: Using Time Out

Session 8: Teaching Children Problem-Solving and Negotiating Skills

Session 9: Learning About Emotion Development

Session 10: Teaching Children to Identify and Label Emotions

Session 11: Handling Children's Negative Emotion: Part One

Session 12: Handling Children's Negative Emotion: Part Two

Session 13: Giving Children Opportunities to Experience Positive Emotion

Session 14: Modeling Emotion Regulation and Expression

Behavior Problems and Normal Development

Being active is normal for a preschooler *but* being much more active than other preschoolers can cause problems. Some children outgrow their hyperactivity, but some do not. Understanding more about attention deficit hyperactivity disorder (ADHD) can be helpful for parents of hyperactive preschoolers regardless of whether their children end up outgrowing their hyperactivity.

What is ADHD?

Symptoms

Difficulty putting the brakes on behavior, much more than other kids of the same age which causes problems with:

- Hyperactivity
    - For example, can't sit still; runs about or climbs excessively
- Inattention
    - For example, easily distracted
- Impulsivity (acting without thinking)
    - For example, difficulty waiting turn

Causes

ADHD is a genetic disorder, which causes problems in the part of the brain called the *prefrontal cortex*. The prefrontal cortex is responsible for planning and controlling behavior.

Development

Children with ADHD typically begin to show symptoms by the age of 3, although not all preschoolers who are hyperactive will go on to have ADHD.

Key Points for Parents

✓ Hyperactive children *can* pay attention to activities with lots of feedback or to activities that are very interesting.

✓ Just because they can pay attention in certain situations does not mean that you should expect that they can pay attention in other situations.

✓ Hyperactive children often know what to do but have difficulty doing it.

✓ Parents cannot make their children not be hyperactive, but they can help their children's hyperactivity cause fewer problems.

Managing Hyperactive Behavior

Session 1

You can't make your hyperactive child stop being hyperactive. But you can channel your child's hyperactivity.

1. Do you have space in the house where your child can be active without hurting him/herself or someone/something else? If you don't, is there a place you could make into such a space?

    _____

    _____

2. Be clear with yourself and with your child about hyperactive behavior that is okay and hyperactive behavior that is not okay in your house:

HYPERACTIVE BEHAVIOR THAT IS *NOT* OKAY	HYPERACTIVE BEHAVIOR THAT IS OKAY

3. Make a list of activities that your child enjoys that you can direct your child to if he/she is doing something that you don't want him/her to be doing. Include both big movement activities (e.g., setting up an obstacle course; running around outside) and small movement (fidget) activities (e.g., playing with Legos). Make sure that some of the small movement activities are things that you can have on hand in public if you need to give your child something to occupy him/her.

BIG MOVEMENT ACTIVITIES	SMALL MOVEMENT ACTIVITIES

Parenting Beliefs and Values

Session 1

Please think about the questions below and write some brief answers to them on this sheet. You will NOT have to show this to anyone. It is really for your own use, and there will be an opportunity to share your thoughts about these questions during the next session if you wish.

1. What kind of person do you want your child to be when he or she grows up?

   _____

   _____

   _____

2. What kind of parent do you want to be?

   _____

   _____

   _____

3. In what ways do you wish you were different as a parent?

   _____

   _____

   _____

4. What are your beliefs about disciplining children?

   _____

   _____

   _____

5. How do you think your own parents/family have affected how you parent?

   _____

   _____

   _____

6. What is the most difficult thing about being a parent?

   _____

   _____

   _____

What Helps You Parent Effectively?

Session 1

THINGS THAT HELP ME PARENT THE WAY I WANT TO	THINGS THAT MAKE IT MORE DIFFICULT FOR ME TO PARENT THE WAY I WANT TO

Session 2

One of the biggest challenges of being a parent is trying to find balance. Parents sometimes find themselves trying to choose between two opposite approaches when, in fact, it's often best to embrace both! Some examples are:

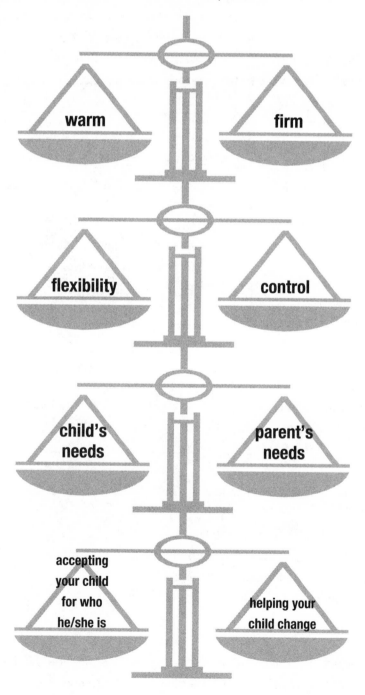

Session 2

Consequences (what happens after a behavior) affect whether that behavior is likely to happen again in the future. Here are some important learning principles that we will come back to throughout the program. These principles can affect your child's behavior *and* your behavior!

Reinforcement

➤ If something good happens after you do something, you are more likely to do it again in the future (e.g., reward)

➤ If something bad goes away after you do something, you are more likely to do it again in the future

Punishment

➤ If something bad happens after you do something, you are less likely to do it in the future

➤ If something good goes away after you do something, you are less likely to do it in the future (e.g., taking away privilege)

How Do You Affect Your Child?

What is one way that you reward your child's good behavior? _____

_____

What is one way that you accidentally reward your child's negative behavior? _____

_____

_____

How Does Your Child Affect You?

What is one way that your child rewards your good parenting behavior? _____

_____

_____

What is one way that your child accidentally rewards your negative parenting behavior? _____

_____

_____

Key Points for Parents

✓ Make sure to reward behavior that you like!

✓ Make sure you don't accidentally reward behavior that you don't like.

✓ Even if you reward a behavior just occasionally, you will see more of that behavior, so be careful about accidentally rewarding behavior. For example, it only takes one laugh for a child to learn to swear.

✓ It's important to be consistent, but it's also very difficult, so "pick your battles."

✓ No parent is perfect. If you find that there is a situation where you can't enforce a rule, be clear with your child that this is a rare exception (and make sure it is!).

Praise

Session 2

Praising children means telling them what you like about their behavior or expressing appreciation for their good behavior.

Catch Me Being Good!!

Why Praise?

➢ It makes it more likely that good behavior will happen again.

➢ It can help children see themselves positively, which in turn leads to emotional well-being and good behavior.

How Should I Praise?

➢ Be specific.
➢ Be genuine—say it like you mean it.
➢ Praise the behavior, not the child.
➢ Praise effort.
➢ Avoid praise that sounds like criticism.

When Should I Praise?

➢ Anytime you notice your child not misbehaving.

How Often Should I Praise?

➢ As often as possible!!

Your Child's Reaction

➢ Most children will be pleased by your praise.

➢ Hyperactive children may get excited and happy and become more hyperactive for a few minutes—do not let this stop you from praising!!

➢ Sometimes children may seem like they don't want you to praise them—don't let this stop you!

Examples: (Fill in the blanks below with some ways you like to praise.)

"I like how nicely you are playing quietly."

"I love how you listened to me the first time I asked you to put on your coat!"

"You hung up your coat on the hook—I really appreciate that."

_____

_____

Catching Your Child Being Good

Session 2

It is often much easier to notice when your child is not behaving well. This week we would like you to make an effort to notice when your child is doing something right or *not* doing something wrong. Because it can be especially hard to notice and praise the absence of bad behavior, try to focus on one or two target behaviors this week:

THINK OF ONE OR TWO MISBEHAVIORS THAT YOU WOULD LIKE TO FOCUS ON THIS WEEK.	WHAT BEHAVIOR WOULD YOU LIKE YOUR CHILD TO DO *INSTEAD* OF THIS MISBEHAVIOR?	WHAT WILL YOU SAY TO YOUR CHILD WHEN YOU NOTICE YOUR CHILD *NOT* DOING THE MISBEHAVIOR?
Example: *Screaming*	Example: *Using a quiet voice*	Example: *"I like how you are talking in a nice quiet voice!"*

Catching Your Child Being Good Log

Session 2

In the chart below keep track of times when your child was *not* engaging in the misbehavior you are focusing on this week.

DAY	TIME	WHAT WAS YOUR CHILD DOING INSTEAD OF THE MISBEHAVIOR?	HOW DID YOU PRAISE YOUR CHILD FOR IT?

Positive Attention

Because hyperactive preschoolers can be difficult to manage, they often receive much more negative attention than positive attention. Although most children prefer positive attention over negative attention, they prefer some attention over no attention at all. In fact, preschoolers often enjoy getting a reaction from adults, even if it is a negative reaction. Increasing the positive attention you give to your child can help satisfy their need for attention and decrease their efforts to seek negative attention. Here are some ways of giving positive attention:

One-on-One Time

➢ Try to find at least 10 minutes each day to focus on paying attention to your child while he/she is playing.

➢ Do not do other things (e.g., read, fold laundry) during your one-on-one time.

➢ You don't have to be playing with your child. It could be 10 minutes of actively watching your child play, while commenting on and describing what your child is doing.

➢ If your child misbehaves during one-on-one time, simply stop the activity.

➢ If your child is being hyperactive during this time, try not to discourage the hyperactivity unless it is dangerous or disruptive.

Describe Your Child's Activities

➢ Pretend you are the narrator in a play.

➢ Pretend you are a sports announcer.

- Example: "You're drawing a huge castle. Look at those towers!"

Other Ways of Giving Positive Attention

➢ Eye contact

➢ Warm/enthusiastic tone of voice when talking to your child

➢ Being near your child

➢ Physical affection

Finding Time for One-on-One Time

Think about when you can find 10 minutes during each day to focus only on playing with your child or paying attention to your child while he/she is playing.

_____

_____

Using Attention and Ignoring to Shape Your Child's Behavior

Session 3

You can use your attention to encourage your child to behave appropriately. If you respond to your child's behavior with attention (positive or negative), that behavior is likely to occur again. If you respond to your child's behavior by removing attention (ignoring), that behavior is less likely to occur again.

Reward Your Child's Good Behavior with Positive Attention

➢ When your child is behaving well, try to give him/her positive attention.

➢ Note that praise can be part of positive attention, but positive attention is much more than just praising.

Ignore Your Child's Attention-Seeking Negative Behavior

➢ If your child is misbehaving to get attention or a reaction, ignore it! (**Important exception**: Do not ignore dangerous behavior!)

➢ Note that if your child is engaging in a lot of attention-seeking behavior, this is likely a sign that he/she needs more positive attention.

How to Ignore

➢ Don't look at your child or talk to your child or talk about your child.

➢ Walk away if it is safe to do so (but make sure that you can still monitor your child for safety).

➢ If you decide to ignore, you need to stick to it.

➢ Ignore the behavior every time it happens!

Your Child's Reaction

➢ It is not uncommon for children to increase the misbehavior at first when you ignore it, which can make it more difficult to ignore! The behavior should decrease after the initial increase, assuming it is really attention-seeking behavior, so be patient.

What are Some Ways That Your Child Tries to Get Your Attention?

Positive ways: _____

Negative ways:_____

Can you ignore the negative attention-seeking behavior?

Positive Attention Log

Session 3

This week, keep track of your one-on-one time with your child.

DATE	TIME STARTED	TIME ENDED	DESCRIBE ONE-ON-ONE TIME	HOW DID YOUR CHILD REACT?	ANY PROBLEMS?

Playing Games with Preschool Children

Session 3

Playing competitive games can be a big challenge for preschoolers, especially for children who have difficulty with impulse control. Preschoolers are often at a disadvantage when playing with adults or older children and are likely to lose games that involve skill. Furthermore, even in games that don't require skill, the child has at most a 50% chance of winning a game. For a preschool-aged child, these odds can be very discouraging and frustrating and can lead to misbehavior.

You certainly can discourage your child from playing competitive games to avoid these difficulties, but there are also many ways that you can adapt playing games to make it an opportunity for children to learn about competition, fairness, and control, without facing continual failure and frustration. When playing games with preschoolers, many adults believe that it is critical to teach children life's hard lessons about fairness, losing, and cheating. Most preschoolers are not developmentally ready to face these ideas fully. Instead, these ideas should be very gradually introduced. This can be difficult for parents, because they worry that their children will never learn these ideas if they don't learn them early. In fact, quite the opposite is true. Your child is more likely to internalize these ideas if they are introduced gradually. Your child will naturally face these issues when playing games with other children, so you don't need to worry that if you don't teach your child these ideas during your one-on-one time, he/she won't learn them. By giving your child some time and space to explore these ideas in a safe environment, your child will be more ready to take them on in another setting.

The key is to be flexible and keep your own sense of competition in check. The purpose of playing games is to have fun. Forcing children to always follow rules during games and expecting children not to be upset by losing will present too great a challenge for most preschool children. Being generous and flexible with your child during games will help to foster the ability to take other children's perspectives and to be flexible and generous with other children. Note that not all parents can do this. People have different perspectives on game playing; if you don't think that you can be flexible in game playing, please simply avoid playing competitive games with your child during your special one-on-one time.

Making Up Rules

It is perfectly fine for your child to make up new rules in a game, and is a great way to foster creativity. If your child makes rules that favor the child over you, you can use this opportunity as a way of gently beginning to help your child take the perspective of other people. It is important to do this in a calm manner. It also might be helpful to ask your child at the beginning of the game whether she would like to change any of the rules, explaining that it is fine to create new rules at the beginning of the game if they are fair to everyone but that we can't change rules halfway through.

Examples:

"So does that mean I get to roll again if I don't like my roll also?"

"It's fine to change the rules, but I wonder if we can change the rules so that they are fair for both of us?"

Cheating

If your child chooses to play a competitive game during one-on-one time, it is not uncommon for preschoolers to "cheat" during games. Although you ultimately want to teach your child not to cheat, your special one-on-one time is not necessarily the time or place to do so. Cheating is very common at this age and is not an indication that your child is a "bad kid." Children of this age are just beginning to be able to take other children's perspectives. Understanding not to cheat requires this skill, so it's important to be patient with your child. There are several possible ways of handling cheating:

- Simply ignore the cheating and continue playing the game. It's okay for your child to win, even if it's by cheating. There will be plenty of opportunity as your child gets older to learn not to cheat. By making a big deal of it now, you will take away much of the benefit of your special one-on-one time.

- If your child cheats, ask your child if he/she would like to change the rules of the game. For example, if he draws Plumpy in Candyland, which would send him back to the beginning, and he doesn't want to go back to the beginning, you could say, "Shall we make a rule that you are allowed to redraw two times during the game if you don't like the card you get?" This allows your child to have more control over negative things that can happen without setting up the game to be unfair to the other player.

- Tell your child that during your special one-on-one time it's okay if he/she doesn't want to follow the rules or wants to do something that would not be fair to you, but explain that if he/she does that with other children it might make the other children mad or sad.

Making a Level Playing Field

There is an important distinction between "letting your child win" and making an even playing field to adjust for differences in size and maturity. You can call it, "Not playing your hardest." You can even have explicit conversations with your child if he/she is losing—"Do you want me to play my hardest or not?" This way a child can have the experience of winning while still understanding developmental differences in skill.

Session 4

For preschoolers, reward programs (sticker/star charts) can be helpful for establishing new habits or patterns of behavior and breaking out of negative cycles. In these programs, your child will earn stickers/stars and will earn a prize or privilege when he/she has enough stickers/stars.

How Do I Set Up a Reward Program?

➢ **Choose the behavior you want to target.**

- Pick 1 or 2 behaviors at a time, so it isn't overwhelming for your preschooler or you.

- Be specific about the behavior you want to see.

- Focus on what behavior you would like to see instead of what you don't want to see.

➢ **Make a list describing what your child needs to do to earn stickers/stars.**

- Write this even though your child can't read.

- Draw simple pictures next to the words to help your child remember what it says.

➢ **Write down a list of prizes and privileges that your child can earn with the stickers/stars.**
- Rewards do *not* need to be big and expensive.
- Examples of privileges
  - An extra story at bedtime
  - Having a special dessert
  - A small amount of extra TV or computer time
  - Getting to stay up 10 minutes later than usual
  - A special outing
  - Doing a special activity with a parent
- Have a "grab bag" or "prize box"
  - Putting small prizes (toys, craft supplies, temporary tattoos, etc.) in a special "grab bag" or "prize box" can make these items even more appealing to preschoolers. When your child has earned enough stickers, he/she gets to pick a prize out of the grab bag or prize box.

➢ **Create a chart or path where you can place stickers/stars that your child has earned.**
- Pace the steps correctly. Try not to make it too hard or too easy to earn stickers/stars and prizes.

How Do I Introduce the Program To My Child?

➢ Pick a time when you and your child are calm and have time to talk and listen.

➢ Introduce the program on a positive note.

➢ Show your child the chart.

➢ Explain what is expected in order to earn a sticker/star.

➢ Involve your child by letting him/her decorate the chart, select the stickers to earn, etc.

➢ Get your child's input (within reason) about what to earn.

➢ End on a positive note.

Key Points for Parents

✓ Give stickers/stars and rewards as soon as possible after the good behavior.

✓ Remember, appropriate behavior, then reward.

✓ Some younger preschoolers may have difficulty understanding the system; you may need to simplify it, or wait till your child is a bit older.

✓ For older children you can make the program more complex (e.g., 2 stars for "super-cooperating," 1 star for "mostly cooperating.")

Session 4

What I'm Working On: <u>Getting ready for preschool in the morning.</u>

What Can I Get with My Stickers?

5 stickers: special snack in the car

★★★★★ =

10 stickers: choose from the prize box.

★★★★★
★★★★★ =

How Can I Earn Stickers?

Each morning I will get 1 sticker for doing each of these things. (So I can earn up to 5 stickers each morning.)

☐ Getting dressed

☐ Eating breakfast

☐ Brushing hair and teeth

☐ Putting on coat and shoes

☐ Getting in the car

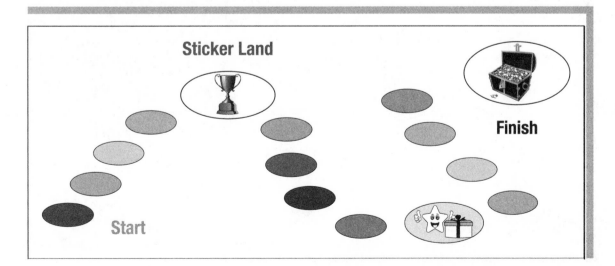

Sticker Land

Start

Finish

What I'm Working On:

_____

_____

What Can I Get with My Stickers?

5 stickers: _____

☆☆☆☆☆ =

10 stickers: _____

☆☆☆☆☆ =

☆☆☆☆☆

How Can I Earn Stickers/stars?

☐ _____

_____

☐ _____

_____

☐ _____

_____

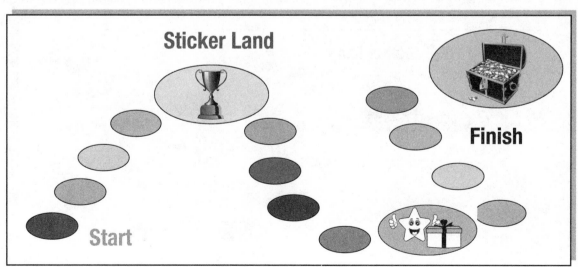

Sticker Land

Start

Finish

Other Types of Reward Charts

Behavior	MONDAY	TUESDAY	WEDNESDAY	THURSDAY	FRIDAY	SATURDAY	SUNDAY	Stickers on ___ days = a prize

Daily Reward Charts

	Get dressed	Eat breakfast	Brush teeth	Get on coat and shoes	Get in car	Total stars		1 star = 1 small treat
Sunday								
Monday								
Tuesday								
Wednesday								
Thursday								
Friday								
Saturday								

What Is Your Style of Giving Commands?

Session 5

Imagine yourself in the following situations and indicate how you would naturally give a command in that situation. (Assume that each situation requires a command—that is, assume that your child is not likely to comply in the situation.)

	WHAT WOULD YOU SAY?	WHAT TONE OF VOICE WOULD YOU USE?	HOW FAR AWAY WOULD YOU BE WHEN YOU GIVE THE COMMAND?
It's time for your child to get dressed in the morning.			
It's time for your child to come to the dinner table.			
Your child is climbing up on the counter.			
It's time for your child to get in the car.			
It's time to leave the playground.			
You want your child to clean up the toys he/she was just playing with.			

What would you like to work on when giving commands? _____

_____

_____

_____

Effective Commands

The way you tell your child to do something will affect whether your child will do what you ask. Use commands ("You need to pick up your toys now.") when it is important that your child obeys and/or when you expect that your child may not obey. Save polite requests ("Could you please pass the salt?") for situations in which obeying is optional or not particularly important.

How Can I Phrase My Commands So They Will Be More Effective?

DO	DON'T
Be clear and specific. ✓ "Put your toy cars away now." ✓ "Come sit in your seat." ✓ "Please use a quieter voice."	**Don't use vague commands.** 🔞 "It's time to clean up." 🔞 "Be good."
Phrase your command as a statement. ✓ "You need to pick up your cars now."	**Don't phrase your command as a question.** 🔞 "Do you want to pick up your toy cars now?"
When possible, tell your child what to do. ✓ "Walk please."	**When possible, avoid telling your child what *not* to do.** 🔞 "Don't run."
Give one command at a time. ✓ "Pick up your toy cars now."	**Don't string commands together.** 🔞 "Pick up your toys, brush your teeth, put on your pajamas, and get in bed."
Give your child time to obey. ✓ "Come here." (pause)	**Don't repeat commands in rapid fire.** 🔞 "Come here! Come here! Come here!"

Key Points for Parents

✓ Try to reduce the number of commands you give.

✓ Only give a command if you are willing to follow through with a negative consequence (if your child doesn't obey) or with a positive consequence (if your child does obey).

✓ Give lead time when you can.

"In 5 minutes it will be time to pick up the toys."

✓ Remind children when transition times are coming.

"When this show is over, it will be time to get ready for bed."

Command Flow Chart

Session 5

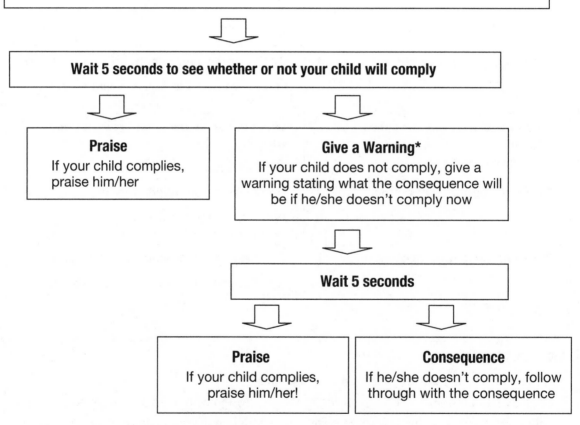

Make sure you have your child's attention
- Stand within 5 feet of your child if possible
- Remove distractions and don't let your child distract you
- Keep eye contact with your child

State your command
- Use a firm tone of voice
- Use a matter of fact, business-like tone, without yelling
- You can say please–just make sure it is a statement rather than a question
- You may pair your command with a brief reason, but be sure to keep it short or your child will tune you out

Wait 5 seconds to see whether or not your child will comply

Praise
If your child complies, praise him/her

Give a Warning*
If your child does not comply, give a warning stating what the consequence will be if he/she doesn't comply now

Wait 5 seconds

Praise
If your child complies, praise him/her!

Consequence
If he/she doesn't comply, follow through with the consequence

*Note that sometimes it may be helpful to first offer a logical reward for complying. These should be privileges rather than prizes. If the child does not respond to your offer, then give a warning for a consequence. Example: "If you start brushing your teeth by time I count to 5, I will have time to read you an extra story tonight." (If the child does not respond, then follow up with a warning: "If you don't start brushing your teeth by the time I count to 5, then you will lose one story tonight.")

Adapted from Danforth, J. S. (2007). Training parents of children with comorbid Attention-Deficit/Hyperactivity Disorder and Oppositional Defiant Disorder. In J. M. Briesmeister, C. E. Schaefer (Eds.), *Handbook of parent training: Helping parents prevent and solve problem behaviors* (3rd ed.) (pp. 345–378). Hoboken, NJ, US: John Wiley & Sons Inc.

Commands Log

Session 5

This week notice how you give commands by filling out the chart below:

WHAT DID YOU WANT YOUR CHILD TO DO?	WHAT DID YOU SAY?	WHAT TONE OF VOICE DID YOU USE?	HOW FAR AWAY WERE YOU WHEN YOU GAVE THE COMMAND?	DID YOU WAIT 5 SECONDS AFTER GIVING THE COMMAND?	WHAT HAPPENED NEXT?

Natural and Logical Consequences and Rewards

Session 6

Because hyperactive children are often impulsive, consequences and rewards can be a powerful tool for helping them put the brakes on their behavior. Hyperactive children are very sensitive to immediate feedback from their environment, so setting up their environment the right way can encourage good behavior.

Natural Consequences and Rewards

➤ Natural consequences and rewards follow naturally from your child's actions if you do not intervene. You simply need to be careful to allow these to occur without interfering.
  - If your child breaks a toy by being too rough, the natural consequence is that your child no longer has that toy. If you don't replace the toy, the natural consequence will have an effect.
  - If your child shares a toy with another child, the natural reward is that the other child might be more likely to share with your child. You don't need to do anything for this to have an effect, though it may be helpful to point out this natural reward to your child.

Logical Consequences and Rewards

➤ Logical consequences and rewards involve *you* giving or removing privileges or items that are logically tied to the behavior.
  - If your child writes on the wall with crayons, the logical consequence might be not being able to use the crayons for the rest of the day.
  - If your child gets ready for bed quickly, the logical reward might be that you read an extra book with your child before turning out the light.

How Can I Make Consequences and Rewards More Effective?

DO	DON'T
✓ Make them as immediate as possible. They should occur that day or the next day if at all possible.	Don't make consequences overly harsh or punitive. Generally avoid giving consequences that will last longer than one day.
✓ Follow through. If you warn your child about a consequence or offer a reward, make sure you do it!	Don't threaten a consequence or offer a reward that you wouldn't actually give. Example: *Don't threaten to leave your child somewhere.*
✓ Make sure rewards and consequences are things your child cares about.	Don't choose consequences or rewards that will be difficult for you to enforce.
✓ Be straightforward and assertive about enforcing consequences or about not giving a reward that a child has not earned.	Don't apologize for giving a consequence or not giving a reward (though it is fine to empathize with your child's disappointment).
✓ Expect your child to test limits.	Don't give in when your child tests limits that you have firmly set.

Give It a Positive Spin

You often have a choice between removing a privilege (giving a consequence) and giving a privilege (giving a reward). Whenever possible, state what the behavior is that you want to see and what the privilege will be if your child does it. For example, instead of saying, "If you don't eat your veggies, you can't have dessert," say, "If you eat your veggies, you can have dessert."

Session 6

In the chart below, list common misbehaviors for your child and what consequences or rewards you might try at home. (When possible, make the consequences or rewards logical; but if there is not an obvious logical consequence or reward, it is fine to use one that is not logically tied to the behavior.)

Examples

BEHAVIOR	CONSEQUENCE OR REWARD	WHAT YOU MIGHT SAY
Come to dinner when called	Dessert	"If you come to the table by the time I count to 5, you can have dessert tonight."
Getting ready in the morning	Video	"If you can get ready for preschool by 7:45, you can watch 15 minutes of your video."
Saying mean things	Going to bed early/ staying up later	"When you say mean things that makes me think you are tired. If I hear you say a mean thing again, you will have to go to bed 15 minutes earlier tonight."
Cleaning up toys	Getting out a new toy	"You can't get out a new toy to play with until you clean up the one you played with last."
Getting ready for bed	Reading extra stories	"If you cooperate with getting ready for bed, we can read an extra story tonight."

Your List

BEHAVIOR	CONSEQUENCE OR REWARD	WHAT WILL YOU SAY?

Consequences and Rewards Log

Session 6

Please keep track of the rewards and consequences you use this week. You do not have to write down *every* time you use a reward or consequence—just pick some examples during the week.

DATE	CHILD'S BEHAVIOR	CONSEQUENCE OR REWARD YOU USED	NATURAL OR LOGICAL?	HOW DID YOUR CHILD REACT?	HOW DID YOU REACT OR FEEL?

Preparing for Time Out

When should I use time out?

➤ For severe misbehaviors, like aggression

What will I need?

➤ A quiet, boring area of the house

➤ A timer

➤ A list of backup consequences

- Examples:
  - no more TV for the day
  - no dessert
  - go to bed early

How long should time out be?

➤ One to three minutes for preschoolers

Where should time out be?

➤ Any quiet, boring place

- Examples:
  - the bottom of the stairs
  - a hallway
  - a couch or chair

Giving warnings for time out

➤ For misbehavior that does not involve aggression and destruction, you can give a warning for time out. However, only give one warning, and be prepared to follow through!

Introducing time out to your child

➤ If you have never used time out, it may help to explain what will happen before he/she misbehaves.

- "I don't like it when you hit me, so from now on, whenever you hit me you will have to go to time out for 3 minutes. Here is where you will have your time out. I won't be able to talk to you while you are in time out. If you get out of time out, then you will (say the backup consequence)."

➤ If you have used time out before but it has been very different from this, then explain how it will be different.

During Time Out

What should I do during time out?

➤ Stay just close enough that you can keep an eye on your child (preferably out of sight).

➤ Avoid looking at or talking to your child.

What do I do if my child screams/tantrums?

➤ Ignore it unless the timer has beeped, in which case you can remind your child every 5 minutes that he/she needs to be quiet to end time out.

➤ If your child has been in time out for 15 minutes, you can lower your expectations for how long your child needs to be quiet.

What do I do if my child swears or says mean and horrible things during time out?

➤ Ignore it!

What do I do if my child dances, sings, or talks about how much he/she likes being in time out?

➤ Ignore it!

Ending Time Out

➤ When the timer beeps, if your child is not screaming, say, "You can get out of time out now." If it is appropriate, you can now work on resolving the situation that led to the misbehavior.

Giving Time Out in Public

➤ Wait until time out is well established at home.

➤ Find the quietest, most boring place you can find.

- In the car
  - Make sure you are in the car or just outside of the car with the child. IMPORTANT NOTE: Only use this location if it is not too hot or too cold in the car.
- Outside a store against a boring wall

Time Out Step-By-Step

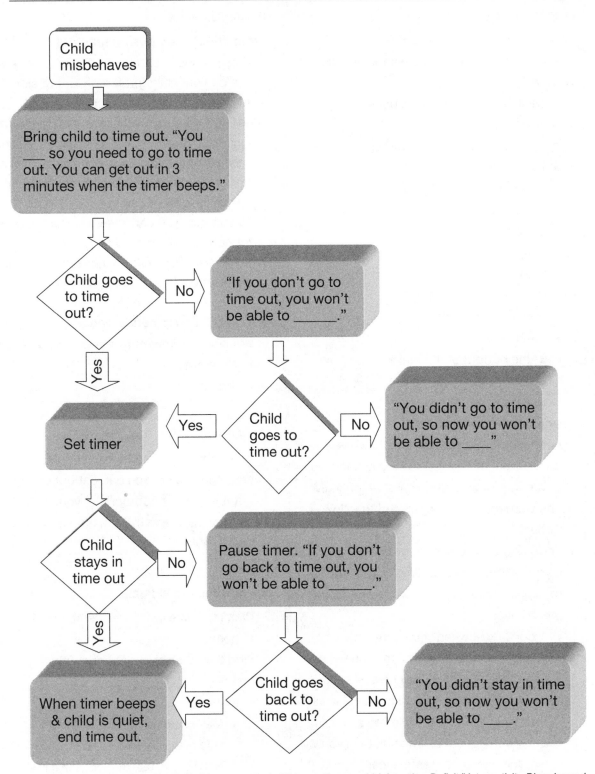

Child misbehaves

Bring child to time out. "You ___ so you need to go to time out. You can get out in 3 minutes when the timer beeps."

Child goes to time out?

No → "If you don't go to time out, you won't be able to _____."

Yes ↓

Set timer

Child goes to time out?

Yes → Set timer

No → "You didn't go to time out, so now you won't be able to ____"

Child stays in time out

Yes ↓

No → Pause timer. "If you don't go back to time out, you won't be able to _____."

Child goes back to time out?

Yes → When timer beeps & child is quiet, end time out.

No → "You didn't stay in time out, so now you won't be able to ____."

When timer beeps & child is quiet, end time out.

Adapted from Danforth, J. S. (2007). Training parents of children with comorbid Attention-Deficit/Hyperactivity Disorder and Oppositional Defiant Disorder. In J. M. Briesmeister, C. E. Schaefer (Eds.), *Handbook of parent training: Helping parents prevent and solve problem behaviors* (3rd ed.) (pp. 345–378). Hoboken, NJ, US: John Wiley & Sons Inc.

Time Out Log

Session 7

WHAT BEHAVIORS WILL YOU USE TIME OUT FOR?		WHERE WILL TIME OUT BE?		WHAT WILL BE YOUR BACKUP CONSEQUENCES?	
DATE	CHILD'S MISBEHAVIOR	WHAT DID YOU SAY?		HOW DID YOUR CHILD REACT?	ANY PROBLEMS?

Session 8

Problem Solving

Define the Problem

➤ Ask your child, "What is the problem?"

➤ If your child is too upset to be able to state the problem, you can state it yourself.

- "It looks like you're unhappy because your brother is playing with something you want. Is that right?"

➤ You don't have to agree with your child that there is a legitimate problem. Simply state the problem from your child's point of view.

➤ If there are two children involved, state the problem from each child's perspective (if there are two perspectives).

Help Your Child Generate Solutions

➤ Ask, "How can we solve this problem?"

➤ If your child expresses an idea, simply restate the idea so that your child knows that you heard him/her. Don't criticize the idea yet.

➤ If your child has a good idea, congratulate your child.

➤ If your child isn't able to come up with any reasonable solutions, suggest some.

➤ Once you have a few reasonable ideas, ask your child which idea he/she likes best.

- If your child likes an idea that does not seem reasonable, say what you like about the idea, but then explain why you think the idea won't work.

➤ At first, you may simply be modeling the problem-solving process for your child.

Teaching Negotiating Skills

Teach Your Child to Negotiate with Others

➤ Give your child suggestions for negotiating.

- "Do you want to bring this toy to John to see if he would like to trade?"

Teach Your Child to Negotiate with You

➤ When your child does not want to do something, and there is a reasonable compromise, prompt your child to suggest a compromise.

- "I see that you don't want to go to bed, but whining is not a good way to get what you want. You do have to go to bed soon, but you could try asking me nicely if you can stay up for 5 more minutes."

➤ If your child negotiates nicely with you, but the request is not reasonable, acknowledge your child's efforts.

- "I really like the way you are asking me if you can have just a small cookie, but I really am worried that even a small cookie will ruin your dinner. You can have a cookie after dinner."

Talking Through Situations in Advance

➤ Problem-solve with your child when you are not in the middle of the problem.

- "I've noticed that we've had problems in the mornings getting ready for school. I end up getting frustrated and yelling, which isn't fun for either of us. I wonder if we can figure out how to solve this problem?"

➤ Remind your child about expectations and consequences/rewards in problem situations.

- "We are going to the store and I really like shopping with you when you cooperate. So remember, there is no screaming in the grocery store and you need to stay in the grocery cart. If you cooperate, you can choose one small thing for us to buy at the end of the trip."

Teaching Problem Solving and Negotiating Log

Session 8

Use this log to record two problem-solving sessions with your child. One session should involve a common problem that you will talk about ahead of time with your child. The other should involve something that comes up spontaneously.

Use this table to describe a problem that came up spontaneously:

DESCRIBE THE SITUATION	HOW WAS THE PROBLEM DEFINED, AND WHO DEFINED IT?	SOLUTIONS THAT YOUR CHILD SUGGESTED	SOLUTIONS THAT YOU SUGGESTED	SOLUTION YOU CHOSE

Use this table to describe a problem that you talked about ahead of time with your child:

DESCRIBE THE PROBLEM	SOLUTIONS THAT YOUR CHILD SUGGESTED	SOLUTIONS THAT YOU SUGGESTED	SOLUTION YOU CHOSE

Session 9

Emotional Competence

➤ Major developmental tasks for preschoolers include learning to:
  • *understand emotions* (identify, label, predict emotions)
  • *express emotions*
  • *regulate emotions* (manage/control emotions)

Emotions

➤ Emotions can be positive or negative and the intensity with which we feel them can vary.

➤ It is common to want to experience positive emotions as much as possible and negative emotions as little as possible, but both positive and negative emotions are important in our lives.

EMOTION	HOW CAN THIS EMOTION BE HELPFUL?
Fear	
Anger	
Sadness	
Happiness	

Key Points for Parents

✓ Children can vary in which emotions they feel in a given situation, how intensely they feel the emotions, and how they express their emotions.

✓ Children don't always know why they feel the way they do.

✓ Children may express one emotion, but it is driven by another emotion.

✓ Just because you would react differently to a certain situation doesn't mean that your child's reaction is wrong or invalid.

✓ Emotions are often not rational, especially for children. Just because an emotion is not rational does not make it any less real and does not make it wrong. Believing that you are wrong for feeling a certain way can often make you feel worse.

Session 9

Brain Development and Emotion
Amygdala

➢ The part of the brain that is strongly associated with emotion is called the amygdala and is already mature at birth.

Cognitive Abilities that Help Regulate Emotion

➢ *Executive function.* The prefrontal cortex is like the control tower of the brain and can also help us control our emotional responses.
➢ *Language.* Language is often used to help regulate emotion.
➢ *Reasoning.* The way we think about an event can affect the way we feel about it.

Cognitive abilities responsible for regulating emotion—particularly executive function—develop much later than the ability to experience emotion, which is why young children often have difficulty regulating their emotions.

Right from Birth, Infants Can Experience Basic Emotions
Ages At Which Emotions Develop

BIRTH	1 MONTH	2 MONTHS	3 MONTHS	4 MONTHS	5 MONTHS	6 MONTHS
Contentment			Joy			
Interest						
Surprise						
Distress			Sadness			Fear
			Disgust			
Frustration				Anger		

From: Lewis, M. (2008). The emergence of human emotions. *Handbook of Emotions (3rd Ed.).*, 304–319.

Hyperactive Preschoolers and Emotion Regulation

➢ Hyperactive preschoolers have difficulty controlling their emotions for the same reasons they have difficulty controlling their behavior—the "control tower" of their brain is not fully developed.

Emotion Beliefs, Values, and Goals

Session 9

People tend to have strong feelings about emotion and emotion expression, particularly when it comes to negative emotions. As we go through life, we get a lot of messages about emotion expression. This is especially true during childhood, when we tend to express emotions more. To help our children with their emotional development, it can be helpful to think about our own beliefs and values about emotions and what messages we want to send our children.

What messages did you receive when you were young about expressing emotions?

_____

_____

_____

What messages do you want to send your child about emotion?

_____

_____

_____

What are your goals for your child's emotional development?

_____

_____

_____

How do you react when your child expresses negative emotions?

_____

_____

_____

How would you like to react when your child expresses negative emotions?

_____

_____

_____

Emotion Log

Session 9

This week we would like you to simply notice the ways that you react to your child's emotions. On 4 days this week, record at least one instance in which your child was expressing emotion (either positive or negative) and describe how you reacted.

DATE	TIME	WHAT EMOTION DO YOU THINK YOUR CHILD WAS EXPERIENCING?	HOW WAS YOUR CHILD EXPRESSING THIS EMOTION?	HOW DID YOUR CHILD'S EMOTION EXPRESSION MAKE YOU FEEL?	HOW DID YOU RESPOND TO THE EMOTION?

Teaching Children to Identify and Label Emotions

Session 10

Emotion knowledge (being able to identify one's own emotions and other people's emotions) is the foundation of being able to control one's own emotions. Learning how to identify and label the emotions of other people is also an important part of your child developing empathy for others. The preschool years are a time of incredible growth in children's emotion knowledge, and as a parent you can play a key role in helping your child identify and talk about emotions.

How Can I Help My Child Learn to Identify and Label Feelings?

- Label your child's emotions when he/she is experiencing them.
  - "You seem very frustrated."
  - "Are you feeling sad, or mad, or both?"
- Label your own emotions in front of your child.
  - "That makes me so happy."
  - "I'm getting frustrated with how long this is taking."
- Label or talk about the emotions of others (siblings, playmates, characters in books and on TV).
  - "Wow, she was really surprised!"
  - "It looks like that hurt his feelings."
  - "That really made her mad, didn't it?"

Key Points for Parents

- ✓ When labeling your child's emotions, try not to sound judgmental or critical. Your tone should be respectful, even if you are not feeling particularly understanding in that moment.
- ✓ After you label your child's emotion, try not to say anything else for a moment (count to 5 in your head) to let what you've said sink in.
- ✓ When labeling your own emotions, you want to let your child understand that you experience a variety of emotions without burdening your child with feeling responsible for your well-being. So use this approach in moderation.
- ✓ When labeling the emotions of others, remember that preschoolers are just developing empathy and that it is normal for preschoolers to still put their own needs before others' needs.

Teaching Children to Identify and Label Emotions

Session 10

Think about the situations below and write down what your first reaction would usually be and what you could say to label your child's emotions.

SITUATION	WHAT WOULD I USUALLY SAY?	WHAT COULD I SAY TO LABEL THE EMOTION?
Your child is doing a difficult puzzle and suddenly throws a puzzle piece across the room.		
You tell your child he/she can't have another cookie and he/she falls down on the floor screaming.		
Your child finishes a puzzle and looks pleased and says, "I'm so good at puzzles!"		
Another child takes a toy away from your child and your child starts crying.		
Your child is having a tantrum and you are not sure why.		
A friend comes to visit and your child starts bouncing off the walls.		
Your child falls down and starts crying, but you don't think it really hurt.		
Your child runs into your room during a thunderstorm and climbs in bed with you.		

Session 10

Emotion expression comes naturally to most children, but their natural ways of expressing emotion—particularly in the case of negative emotion—may not be appropriate and may cause problems in their interactions with others. Children are not born knowing how to express emotions in appropriate ways—parents need to teach them.

How Can I Teach My Child Good Ways of Expressing Emotion?

➤ Labeling of emotions is an important first step in teaching good ways of expressing emotions.

➤ You can teach children good ways of expressing emotions by suggesting alternatives when they are expressing emotion in an inappropriate way.

- "I can see that you are very angry." (wait 5 seconds) "You may not call me names or throw things when you are angry, but you can say, 'You're making me so mad!!' and stomp your foot."

- When they do express emotions in appropriate ways, praise them!

➤ You can also teach children ways of expressing emotions by brainstorming good alternatives when you are not in the heat of the moment.

- "I noticed that when you get really angry, you start throwing things. When you throw things you break things and make a mess, so that's not okay. Let's think of things that you can do instead when you are really mad."

What Are Some Good Ways of Expressing Emotions That You Can Suggest to Your Child?

Examples: "I'm so mad!" . . . "This is frustrating!"

_____

_____

_____

_____

➤ We eventually want to teach children to express their anger through words rather than physical force. But for a child who is expressing emotion physically, it may be helpful to suggest physical expressions of emotion that are safe and nondestructive, like stomping feet or punching a pillow. You can then gradually replace these with verbal expressions of emotion.

➤ Sit down with your child and fill out the chart on the next page to identify good ways your child can express emotion. It may be helpful to draw pictures to go with the words you write.

Session 10

WHEN I'M FEELING…	✓ I CAN SHOW HOW I FEEL BY…	ⓘ I SHOULD TRY NOT TO …

Labeling Feelings Log

This week, please try to label your child's feelings at least twice a day. Remember, when you label your child's feelings, pause for at least 5 seconds afterward before saying anything else.

DO	DON'T
"I can see how angry you are." (5 second pause) "I know that you are angry, but you can't talk to me that way. You can say, 'I'm really mad' and stomp your foot when you are mad."	"I can see how angry you are, but you can't talk to me that way. You say, 'I'm really mad' and stomp your foot when you are mad." (This parent did not wait a few seconds after labeling, before correcting the child.)
"You are really getting frustrated, aren't you?"	"I know you're upset, but there's nothing to be upset about."

DATE	WHAT DID YOU SAY?	DID YOU PAUSE AFTER LABELING?	HOW DID YOUR CHILD REACT?

Validating Negative Emotion

Emotions like anger, sadness, frustration, and anxiety are a normal part of life, especially for preschoolers. Most parents' first instinct is to try to make negative emotions go away. Changing the way you approach your child's negative emotions can help you use emotional outbursts as an opportunity to teach your child about emotion and develop his/her emotional competence.

How to Validate Negative Emotion

Validating your child's emotions means acknowledging and accepting your child's feelings.

Do

➢ Label emotions.
  ● "I can see how angry you are."
➢ Express understanding.
  ● "I can understand how disappointed you are about not being able to have a cookie because I know how much you love cookies."
➢ Directly tell your child that it's okay to feel the way he/she is feeling.
  ● "It's okay to feel sad/mad/frustrated."
➢ Simply be with children quietly while they are experiencing negative feelings.
➢ Let children know that negative emotions can be very intense while you are having them, but they do pass with time. This sends the message that feelings are normal and also gives children a way of coping with strong feelings.
  ● "When I feel really upset, I find that if I just let myself feel upset for a little while, the sad or mad feelings start to get smaller by themselves after a while."

Don't

➢ Hurry to fix their negative feelings.
➢ Tell your child to stop feeling the way they are feeling.

Why Validate Emotion?

➢ When people invalidate our feelings, it tends to make our feelings more intense.
➢ One of the best ways of moving on is to accept feelings, even if they aren't rational.

Things to Think About

➢ You don't have to agree with your child to validate his/her feelings.
➢ Validating your child's feelings does not mean that you are going to give in to your child.
  ● "I can understand how disappointed you are about not being able to have a cookie." (pause) "But you can't have a cookie before dinner because it's not good for you."
➢ Try to be genuine.
  ● This means trying to put yourself in your child's shoes, not as a rational adult but imagining yourself as a preschooler.
➢ Feeling emotions is not a misbehavior.

After you have validated your child's feelings (and only after!), there are a number of things you can do to help your child calm down. Some approaches are best used during more intense emotion and others are best used during less intense emotion.

Give Your Child Time and/or Space

- Walk away from your child.
- Be with your child physically, and either say nothing or continue to validate your child's feelings.
- It can be helpful to say what you are doing so that you can begin to give children language for asking for space when they need it.
  - "I can see how upset you are, so I'm going to give you some space to calm down."

How do I know when to walk away?

Sometimes children need to be left alone, and sometimes children need company when they're feeling negative emotions.

- Use trial and error.
- Ask your child if he/she wants to be left alone.
- Sometimes it's helpful to walk away for a little while and then come back again.
- Pay attention to what you need as a parent.

What if I can't give my child time or space?

In some cases your child is really upset and needs time to calm down, but you don't have the luxury of just giving him/her space.

- Examples:
  - You are about to leave for work/preschool
  - You are in public
- It is fine to move children while they are upset (put them in the car, move to a location where the screaming won't disturb others)—just be careful not to hurt them.
- Give your child "verbal space."
  - Quietly go about what you need to do.

Other Things You Can Do

- Distraction
  - Be careful not to jump to distraction too quickly.
  - It may be helpful to let your child be upset for 5 minutes, and if he/she has not calmed down you can try distraction.
  - Be careful not to reward your child's tantrum by giving something special whenever he/she is upset.
  - Distracting with activities is generally better than distracting with treats.
- Suggest taking deep breaths (and breathe with your child!)
- Count to 10
  - "Let's count to 10 to try to help ourselves calm down. 1...2..."
- Sing

Things to Think About

- Watch your child for cues for what works best.
- If you try to help your child calm down and it isn't working, give your child more time and try again later.
- If there are situations that you anticipate will make your child upset, talk through with your child ways to help prepare.

Validating Emotion and Helping Your Child Calm Down Log

Session 11

Keep track this week of times when your child was upset and how you handled it.

DATE	WHAT WAS YOUR CHILD UPSET ABOUT?	HOW DID YOU VALIDATE YOUR CHILD'S FEELINGS?	HOW DID YOUR CHILD REACT?	WHAT DID YOU DO TO HELP YOUR CHILD CALM DOWN?	HOW DID YOUR CHILD REACT?

Session 12

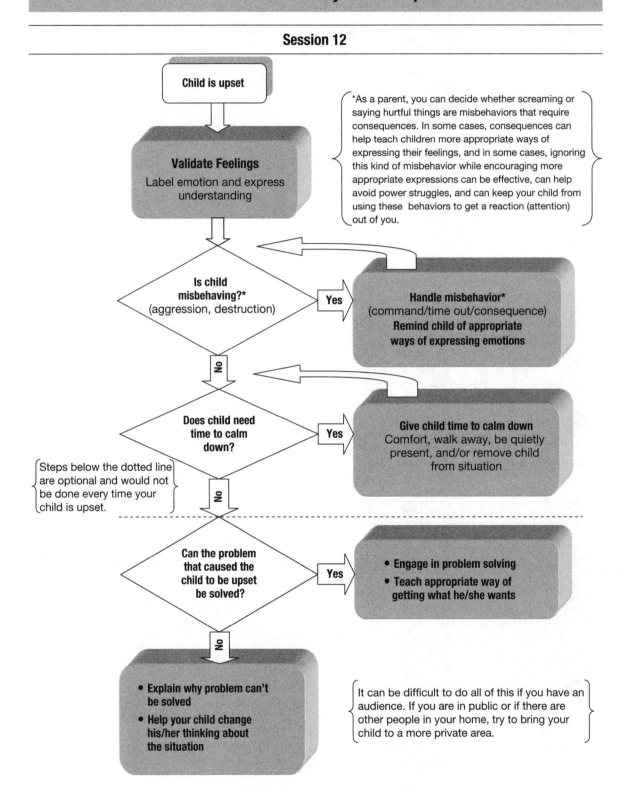

Child is upset

Validate Feelings
Label emotion and express understanding

*As a parent, you can decide whether screaming or saying hurtful things are misbehaviors that require consequences. In some cases, consequences can help teach children more appropriate ways of expressing their feelings, and in some cases, ignoring this kind of misbehavior while encouraging more appropriate expressions can be effective, can help avoid power struggles, and can keep your child from using these behaviors to get a reaction (attention) out of you.

Is child misbehaving?*
(aggression, destruction)

Yes

Handle misbehavior*
(command/time out/consequence)
Remind child of appropriate ways of expressing emotions

No

Does child need time to calm down?

Yes

Give child time to calm down
Comfort, walk away, be quietly present, and/or remove child from situation

Steps below the dotted line are optional and would not be done every time your child is upset.

No

Can the problem that caused the child to be upset be solved?

Yes

- **Engage in problem solving**
- **Teach appropriate way of getting what he/she wants**

No

- **Explain why problem can't be solved**
- **Help your child change his/her thinking about the situation**

It can be difficult to do all of this if you have an audience. If you are in public or if there are other people in your home, try to bring your child to a more private area.

Example 1

Session 12

Child: "I want a cookie!"

Parent: "You can't have a cookie now because it's almost dinner. You can have some cheese and crackers if you are hungry."

Child: (Screams and cries) "I want a cookie now!!!" (Kicks parent)

Parent: "I can see how disappointed you are that you can't have a cookie. You may not kick other people, even when you are angry, so you need to go to time out."

Child: "No!!"

Parent: (Gently but firmly carries the child to time out) "You need to stay here until the timer rings."

Child: (Stays in time out but is screaming and crying)

Parent: (Ignores screaming and crying until the timer rings) (Timer rings) "The timer rang, so you can get out of time out as soon as you can be quiet."

Child: (Screams for a few more minutes and then begins to cry more quietly)

Parent: "You can get out of time out now. You may not kick me when you are mad. Next time you are mad, you can say, 'I'm really mad that you said I can't have a cookie!'"

Child: (Lies on the floor crying) "But I really want a cookie!!"

Optional:

Parent: I know how much you really wanted a cookie—cookies are so delicious aren't they? So the problem is that you really want a cookie, but I don't think it's good for your body to eat a cookie before dinner. I wonder how we can solve this problem?"

Child: (Stops crying) "You could give me a cookie!"

Parent: "That would make you happy, wouldn't it? What else could we do?"

Child: "Maybe I could have one bite of a cookie?"

Parent: "Next time you ask me for a cookie and I say, 'No,' that might be a good thing to ask for—and I might say yes. You kicked me when I said no today so that doesn't make me want to give you even a bite of cookie today. But maybe we can think of something that's delicious that is also healthy that you could have. Like some raisins? Or some apple?"

Child: (Sighs) "I guess raisins are ok."

Parent: "Great. I really like how you are talking calmly to me about this now, even though you were so mad before."

What messages has this child been given?

- Screaming and kicking does not get me what I want.
- I can't always get what I want, but next time if I ask nicely and negotiate, I might get part of what I want.
- It's normal to feel disappointed when I don't get what I want, but it's not ok to hurt people when I am upset (and there will be a consequence if I do).
- It's possible to act calm even when something upsetting is happening (parent is demonstrating this).

Example 2

You are at the grocery store checkout line and you are halfway through checking out.

Child: "I want a candy bar."

Parent: "Those look delicious don't they? We already have enough treats at home, so I don't want to buy any candy bars today, but I bought some crackers and you can have some of those in the car."

Child: "But I want a candy bar!" (Lies down on the floor and start screaming)

Parent: (To the cashier) "Just one second." (Bends down next to the child and says quietly, but loud enough for the child to hear) "I can see how disappointed you are. You must really love candy bars."

Child: (Still screaming, nods head)

Parent: (Still bending down, and talking as quietly and calmly as she can) "I understand how disappointing it is, but it's not okay to scream in the grocery store.'"

Child: (Still screaming and lying on the floor)

Parent: (Goes back to checking out and ignores the tantrum) (To the cashier and the person behind them in line) "Sorry. I find it best to ignore his tantrum now and I'll try to get out of here as fast as possible." (Finishes checking out and asks the person bagging groceries). "Do you mind pushing my cart to the car while I carry my child?" (Picks up child still screaming, carries child to the car, and buckles child without saying anything to the child)

Child: (Still crying but no longer screaming) "I hate you!"

Parent: "Wow you are still really mad about the candy bar, aren't you?"

Child: (Nods)

Parent: "It would be nice if we could always get what we wanted, wouldn't it?"

Child: (Nods and still crying)

Optional:

Parent: "There are a lot of times that you do get what you want. Remember yesterday you got to have a special dessert? But today was a day that you didn't get what you wanted, and I know that it's really disappointing. It's fine to tell me how mad and disappointed you are, but it's not okay to scream in the grocery store. I'm a lot more likely to get you special treats if you can use your words to tell me when you're mad instead of screaming at me."

What messages has this child been given?

- Screaming does not get me what I want.
- Sometimes I get things I want, and sometimes I don't.
- It's normal to feel upset when I don't get what I want, but I need to try use calm words to say how I'm feeling instead of screaming.
- It's possible to act calm even when something upsetting is happening (parent is demonstrating this).

Helping Children Change Thoughts

Session 12

The way we think about a situation can often affect how we feel about it. Although children's feelings are often not rational, you can begin the process of teaching them to change how they feel by changing the way they think.

Focus On the Positive
➢ "That was a sad thing that happened in your day. Were there other happy things that happened to you today?"

Help Them Put Themselves in Another Person's Shoes
➢ Your child is sad because another child did not want to play: "I know that sometimes you are not in the mood to play with some of your friends, even when you really like those friends, but then the next day you are often in the mood to play with them again. I wonder if they felt the same way."

Explain That Sometimes We Get Our Way and Sometimes We Don't
➢ "Sometimes we get to do things our way, and sometimes we don't. If you always got to do things your way, then I wouldn't be able to do things my way; and if I always got to do things my way, then you'd never be able to do things your way. So we have to take turns. I'm a grown-up, so I'm the one who decides when it's your turn to get what you want—but I do my best to let you do things your way unless I think it's not good for you or unless I think it's not fair to someone else."

Help Them Accept Imperfection
➢ It is common for preschoolers to get upset when their ideas get ahead of their abilities. It is a slow process, but you can begin to help them understand that things don't have to be perfect to be wonderful.

  • "I can see how frustrated you are that your castle isn't coming out the way you want it to." (pause, comfort, give space) "I know that you want it to come out just right, and I love that you have such great ideas about things. But a lot of times we can't quite make things work the way we want them to and we just have to say, "Oh well! Good enough!"

Things To Think About
➢ If you jump in to change children's thinking too quickly, they're likely to resist. Make sure to do this only after you have validated and given them some time to calm down.
➢ Don't have these discussions when your child is experiencing intense emotions. Wait until your child is starting to calm down.
➢ Teaching children to change the way they think about things is a slow, gradual process, so don't expect them to change overnight. You are slowly teaching them ways of coping with upsetting situations.

What Can I Do When My Child Is Upset?

Session 12

SITUATION	WHAT CAN YOU DO TO VALIDATE YOUR CHILD'S EMOTION?	WHAT CAN YOU DO TO HELP YOUR CHILD CALM DOWN?	WHAT CAN YOU SAY TO HELP YOUR CHILD THINK DIFFERENTLY ABOUT THE SITUATION?
Your child is doing a difficult puzzle and suddenly throws a puzzle piece across the room.			
You tell your child he/she can't have another cookie and he/she falls down on the floor screaming.			
Another child takes a toy away from your child and your child starts crying.			
Your child falls down and starts crying, but you don't think it really hurt.			
Your child runs into your room during a thunderstorm and climbs in bed with you.			

Session 12

Fears are extremely common among preschoolers and there are some important things to keep in mind when your child is upset out of anxiety or fear.

Validate and Reassure

➢ First validate your child's fears:

"Thunder sounds really scary to you, doesn't it?"

➢ Then reassure your child that he/she is safe:

"Even though it sounds scary, it can't hurt you. I really like thunder, because it sounds like big trucks driving through the clouds."

Gently Encourage Your Child to Face His/Her Fears

➢ Helping children to face their fears can help them overcome anxiety, and avoiding fears can make them worse. But it's also important to be careful not to push them too hard, because that also can make things worse.

➢ Sometimes it is useful to help your child gradually face fears.

- For example, if your child is afraid of big dogs, try to first arrange for him to play with smaller dogs in safe situations; then have your child be as close to a friendly but large dog as he/she can comfortably be, and then gradually have your child get used to being closer and closer to the large dog.

Give Your Child Time to Outgrow the Fear

➢ Most children outgrow their fears naturally.

- Unless your child's anxiety is causing big problems for you or your child, it's often best to let your child outgrow his/her fears.

- BUT, if your child's anxiety is causing big problems for you or your child, it's good to get assistance from a mental health professional to help with your child's anxiety.

Things to Avoid

🚫 Don't shame your child (e.g., "What's wrong with you?").

🚫 Don't call your child a baby.

🚫 Don't tell your child to be a big boy or big girl when he/she is afraid.

🚫 Don't tell your child he/she is silly for being afraid.

When Your Child Overcomes a Fear

➢ Complement your child on overcoming the fear (without criticizing the earlier fear).

➢ Use this as an opportunity to teach your child that feelings change as we get older.

Handling Your Child's Negative Emotions Log

Session 12

This week when your child gets upset, use the What Do I Do When My Child is Upset? flowchart and record your experiences below.

DATE	WHAT WAS YOUR CHILD UPSET ABOUT?	HOW DID YOU VALIDATE YOUR CHILD'S FEELINGS?	IF YOUR CHILD WAS MISBEHAVING, HOW DID YOU HANDLE IT?	WHAT DID YOU DO TO HELP YOUR CHILD CALM DOWN?	HOW DID IT WORK?

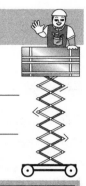

Session 13

Scaffolding

➢ Scaffolds help workers to be right at the level they need to be working—the height of the scaffold can be increased when the worker completes a particular area. Parents are scaffolds for their children—the trick is figuring out the right height of the scaffold so that your child can work on the right area.

➢ Moving too slowly or too quickly are both common. If in doubt, it's better to move too slowly than too quickly.

Things to Think About in Setting Your Child Up for Success

➢ Age comparisons in your praise may help make it feel genuine to you and your child. This makes it clear that there are different expectations for younger children than for older children.

- "Wow, you are really good at soccer for a 4-year-old!"

➢ Adjusting your expectations may mean adjusting your behavior.

- Examples:
  - You may decide that your child really isn't ready to be able to sit in a restaurant, so you may need to not take him/her to restaurants until he/she is ready.
  - You may need to put a high lock on the door if your child leaves the house when he/she should not.

What About When Your Child Doesn't Succeed?

➢ Remind your child that no one is perfect.

➢ Tell your child that it's good to have things that he/she can't do because that means there are things that he/she gets to learn how to do.

➢ Tell your child that he/she has many years to learn how to do it.

➢ Praise your child's effort: "Not quite, but good try!"

➢ Emphasize the difficulty of the task: "Wow that's really hard!"

Example of Scaffolding at Home

Session 13

Think of an activity that is challenging for your child. Make a list of goals within this activity that are easy for your child to accomplish, a little challenging, and very difficult for your child.

Activity: Eating dinner together

EASY	A LITTLE CHALLENGING	VERY DIFFICULT
Sitting in seat while chewing (but getting up between bites)	Sitting at the table for 3 minutes	Sitting at the table for 5 minutes
Standing next to the table while eating	Alternating between sitting and standing at the table for 5 minutes	Alternating between sitting and standing at the table for 10 minutes
Eating hotdogs, macaroni and cheese, grilled cheese	Eating one raw vegetable	Eating one cooked vegetable
Using manners once during the meal (e.g., saying please or thank you)	Using manners three times during the meal	Using manners throughout the meal

> ➢ Your goal is to set the scaffold halfway between easy and a little challenging.
> - 1st week:
>   - Praise your child for tasks he/she accomplishes on the easy list.
>   - Ignore his/her inability to do things on the second and third list.
>   - If your child accomplishes anything on the second or third list, make a big deal of it!
> - 2nd week and beyond:
>   - Continue what you did during the first week, but slowly encourage your child to try things on the second list. Again, make a big deal if he/she is able to do things on the second list, but avoid scolding and criticizing if he/she is unable to do them.

Scaffolding at Home

Session 13

Think of an activity that is challenging for your child at home. Make a list of goals within this activity that are easy for your child to accomplish, a little challenging, and very difficult for your child.

Activity _____

EASY	A LITTLE CHALLENGING	VERY DIFFICULT

> ➤ Your goal is to set the scaffold halfway between easy and a little challenging.
> - 1st week:
>   - Praise your child for tasks he/she accomplishes on the easy list.
>   - Ignore his/her inability to do things on the second and third list.
>   - If your child accomplishes anything on the second or third list, make a big deal of it!
> - 2nd week and beyond:
>   - Continue what you did during the first week, but slowly encourage your child to try things on the second list. Again, make a big deal if he/she is able to do things on the second list, but avoid scolding and criticizing if he/she is unable to do them.

Session 13

Emphasizing Your Child's Strengths

➤ Try to tell your child at least one thing you like about him/her every day.

- This can be very difficult to do if your child is having a hard day. Telling your child things that you like about your child is not the same as excusing his/her bad behavior.
    - Example: "I wasn't very happy with how much you and your brother were fighting today, but I wanted to let you know how much I appreciate what a good big brother you usually are."

Affection/Warmth/Expressing Your Love

➤ It's important to be able to separate your disapproval of your child's behavior from your love of your child. Even though you may know this, your child needs to hear it!

- "Did you know that I love you even when I get mad at you?"
- A parent-child "vow": "Did you know that I love you when you are happy or sad, when you are behaving well and when you are behaving badly, when you are good at doing something and when you have a hard time doing something? No matter what."
- "I didn't like that you weren't listening to me tonight at bedtime, but even when I don't like what you're doing, I still love you."

Helping Children to Look At the Bright Side

➤ The way we view the events in our lives can have a big impact on how we feel about those events. Focusing on the positive rather than the negative aspect of events can often help us feel better about the event.

➤ When you are helping your child focus on the positive, remember that if your child is upset about something it is important to not invalidate the negative aspects of an event. First validate (express understanding, label emotion), and let your child have time to feel your support; then work on helping your child to think differently about the situation.

- Example:
    - Your child skins his/her knee and cries: "Ooh, that looks like it really hurts. I'm so sorry you got hurt." (Give child a chance to cry) "Let's get that cleaned up and put a bandage on it—I bet it will feel better in no time."

My Child's Strengths

Session 13

These are the things I really like about _____

_____

_____

_____

_____

_____

_____

_____

_____

_____

_____

_____

Session 13

Try to tell your child at *least* one thing you like about him/her every day.

DATE	WHAT DID YOU SAY TO YOUR CHILD?	WHAT WAS YOUR CHILD'S REACTION?	HOW DID YOU FEEL?

Session 14

Managing Your Own Emotions

➢ The goal is not to stop you from experiencing strong emotions—having strong emotional reactions is natural when you are a parent. The goal is to figure out how to manage them when you do have them.

➢ Everyone finds different things helpful. Some strategies that parents often find helpful include:

- Count to 10
- Take slow deep breaths
- Take a break away from your child (making sure child is safe and monitored)
- Exercise
- Talk with someone (call a friend)
- Tell yourself calming statements

➢ Change the way you think about the situation.

- *What are some thoughts that you often have when you are angry and what might be another way to think about the situation?*

INSTEAD OF THINKING...	YOU MIGHT THINK...
Examples:	
What's wrong with my child?!	All children are different and have their own challenges.
My child is being a brat.	It's normal for children to want to have things their way. It's my job to teach my child that he/she can't always have his/her own way.

➢ Talk to your child about your strategies for managing your emotions.

- "I'm really angry right now so I'm going to go in the other room for a few minutes to calm down. I'll be out in a few minutes."

Take Care of Your Own Emotional Well-Being

On airplanes we are often instructed to put on our own oxygen masks before helping our children put on theirs. This is because we need to be able to function ourselves in order to help our children.

What things can you do to help yourself feel less stressed?

_____

_____

Express Your Own Emotions in Healthy Ways

➤ Label your own feelings as calmly as possible.

➤ Tell others how you feel without lashing out at them.

   • Use "I" statements: "I feel frustrated when I feel like I'm the only one in the house cleaning up." (instead of, "How many times do I have to tell you to clean up after yourself?")

   • Try to avoid sarcasm, belittling, and saying mean things when you are angry.

➤ If you are so upset that you don't think you can express yourself in a healthy way, try to simply say nothing!

Talk With Your Child About Your Own Efforts to Control the Way You Are Expressing Your Emotions

➤ "Right now I'm angry and feel like yelling, but I'm going to try not to."

Apologize If You Did Something You Regret

➤ "Even though I was upset, it is not ok for me to say mean things to you. I am sorry I did that."

➤ Everyone yells sometimes. Our goal is to try not to yell, but not be too hard on ourselves when we do and know that it's a normal part of parenting.

Is It OK to Cry in Front of My Child?

➤ Yes. Crying in front of children teaches them that crying is a normal way of expressing sadness.

➤ *But*, it can be upsetting for children to see their parents crying a lot, so if you find yourself crying a lot, it may be best to try to limit how often your child sees you crying.

➤ It can be helpful to talk with your child about your crying.
   • "I was really sad about our cat dying, but crying helped me get rid of some of the sadness."

Is It OK to Fight With My Child's Other Parent in Front of My Child?

➤ Having adults yell or be mean to each other in front of children can be very upsetting for children, so if you are having this type of fight, it's better to do this behind closed doors.

➤ *But*, it can be very good for children to see their parents work out differences in constructive ways, so do this in front of your child when it's an appropriate topic.

➤ If your child does see you fighting intensely, talk to your child about what he/she saw.

   • "I know you saw me fighting with your dad yesterday and we were both really angry. After you went to bed, we talked through our problem and we are both feeling much better today. Was it upsetting for you to see us fight?"

Session 14

- Praising good behavior
- Catching your child being good (praising the absence of misbehavior)
- Having special one-on-one time
- Ignoring negative attention-seeking behavior
- Using reward charts
- Giving effective commands (firm, calm, business-like tone; be near your child)
- Using logical rewards

- Using logical consequences
- Using time out
- Helping your child problem-solve
- Teaching your child good ways of expressing emotions.
- Labeling emotions
- Validating your child's emotions
- Helping children change how they feel by changing how they think (after validating!)

What Parenting Tools Work Best for You?

Session 14

In this program, we have presented many different tools. Some tools work better for some families than others and some tools that don't work now may work better in the future, so keep them in your toolbox. Think about what tools seem to work well and write them below to remind yourself to keep using them. Also, think about what you want to continue working on as a parent.

What do you want to continue to work on as a parent?

_____

_____

_____

_____

_____

What strategies seem to work best for you and your child?

_____

_____

_____

_____

_____

References

American Psychiatric Association. (2013). *Diagnostic and statistical manual of mental disorders, 5th Edition: DSM-5*. Arlington, VA: American Psychiatric Association.

Bandura, A. (1978). The self system in reciprocal determinism. *American Psychologist, 33*(4), 344–358.

Barkley, R. A. (1997). Behavioral inhibition, sustained attention, and executive functions: Constructing a unifying theory of ADHD. *Psychological Bulletin, 121*, 65–94.

Barkley, R. A. (2006). *Attention-deficit hyperactivity disorder: A handbook for diagnosis and treatment* (3rd ed.). New York, NY: Guilford Press.

Barkley, R. A. (2013). *Defiant children: A clinician's manual for assessment and parent training* (3rd ed.). New York, NY: Guilford Press.

Baumrind, D. (1966). Effects of authoritative parental control on child behavior. *Child Development, 37*, 887–907.

Baumrind, D. (1971). Current patterns of parental authority. *Developmental Psychology Monograph, 4*, 1–102.

Baumrind, D., & Black, A. E. (1967). Socialization practices associated with dimensions of competence in preschool boys and girls. *Child Development, 38*, 291.

Bierman, K. L., Domitrovich, C. E., Nix, R. L., Gest, S. D., Welsh, J. A., Greenberg, M. T., ... Gill, S. (2008). Promoting academic and social-emotional school readiness: The head start REDI program. *Child Development, 79*, 1802–17.

Bloom, B., Cohen, R. A., & Freeman, G. (2012). Summary health statistics for U.S. children: National Health Interview Survey. *National Center for Health Statistics. Vital Health Statistics, 2011, 10*(254). Retrieved from http://www.cdc.gov/nchs/data/series/sr_10/sr10_258.pdf.

Bor, W., Sanders, M. R., & Markie-Dadds, C. (2002). The effects of the Triple P-Positive Parenting Program on preschool children with co-occurring disruptive behavior and attentional/hyperactive difficulties. *Journal of Abnormal Child Psychology, 30*, 571–87.

Bowlby, J. (1983). Attachment and loss: Retrospect and prospect. *Annual Progress in Child Psychiatry & Child Development*, 29–47.

Brownell, C. A., Svetlova, M., Anderson, R., Nichols, S. R., & Drummond, J. (2013). Socialization of early prosocial behavior: Parents' talk about emotions is associated with sharing and helping in toddlers. *Infancy, 18*, 91–119.

Cadesky, E. B., Mota, V. L., & Schachar, R. J. (2000). Beyond words: How do children with ADHD and/or conduct problems process nonverbal information about affect? *Journal of the American Academy of Child and Adolescent Psychiatry, 39*, 1160–7.

Cameron, J., Banko, K. M., & Pierce, W. D. (2001). Pervasive negative effects of rewards on intrinsic motivation: The myth continues. *The Behavior Analyst, 24*, 1–44.

Campbell, S. B. (2002). *Behavior problems in preschool children: Clinical and developmental issues* (2nd ed.). New York, NY: Guilford Press.

Danforth, J. S., Barkley, R. A., & Stokes, T. F. (1991). Observations of parent-child interactions with hyperactive children: Research and clinical implications. *Clinical Psychology Review, 11,* 703–27.

Danforth, J. S., Harvey, E., Ulaszek, W. R., & McKee, T. E. (2006). The outcome of group parent training for families of children with attention-deficit hyperactivity disorder and defiant/aggressive behavior. *Journal of Behavior Therapy and Experimental Psychiatry, 37*(3), 188–205.

Darling, N., & Steinberg, L. (1993). Parenting style as context: An integrative model. *Psychological Bulletin, 113,* 487–96.

Denham, S. A., Bassett, H. H., & Wyatt, T. (2008). The socialization of emotional competence. In J. Gusec & P. Hastings (Eds.), *Handbook of socialization: Theory and research* (pp. 614–37). New York, NY: Guilford Press.

Denham, S. A., & Burton, R. (1996). A social-emotional intervention for at-risk 4-year-olds. *Journal of School Psychology, 34,* 225–45.

Denham, S. A., Mitchell-Copeland, J., Strandberg, K., Auerbach, S., & Blair, K. (1997). Parental contributions to preschoolers' emotional competence: Direct and indirect effects. *Motivation and Emotion, 21,* 65–86.

Domitrovich, C. E., Cortes, R. C., & Greenberg, M. T. (2007). Improving young children's social and emotional competence: A randomized trial of the preschool "PATHS" curriculum. *The Journal of Primary Prevention, 28,* 67–91.

DuPaul, G. J., & Kern, L. (2013). Comparison of parent education and functional assessment-based intervention across 24 months for young children with attention deficit hyperactivity disorder. *School Psychology Review, 42,* 56–75.

Egger, H. L., Kondo, D., & Angold, A. (2006). The epidemiology and diagnostic issues in preschool attention-deficit/hyperactivity disorder. *Infants & Young Children, 19*(2), 109–22.

Eisenberg, N., Cumberland, A., & Spinrad, T. L. (1998). Parental socialization of emotion. *Psychological Inquiry, 9*(4), 241–73. Retrieved from http://www.pubmedcentral.nih.gov/articlerender.fcgi?artid=1513625&tool=pmcentrez&rendertype=abstract.

Eisenstadt, T. H., Eyberg, S., McNeil, C. B., Newcomb, K., & Funderburk, B. (1993). Parent-Child Interaction Therapy with behavior problem children: Relative effectiveness of two stages and overall treatment outcome. *Journal of Clinical Child Psychology, 22,* 42–51.

Eyberg, S. M., & Bussing, R. (2010). Parent-child interaction therapy for preschool children with conduct problems. In R. C. Murrihy, A. D. Kidman, & T. H. Ollendick (Eds.), *Clinical handbook of assessing and treating conduct problems in youth* (pp. 139–62). New York, NY: Springer New York.

Fabiano, G. A., Pelham, W. E., Manos, M. J., Gnagy, E. M., Chronis, A. M., Onyango, A. N., … Swain, S. (2004). An evaluation of three time-out procedures for children with attention-deficit/hyperactivity disorder. *Behavior Therapy, 35,* 449–469.

Fanton, J. H., MacDonald, B., & Harvey, E. A. (2008). Preschool parent-pediatrician consultations and predictive referral patterns for problematic behaviors. *Journal of Developmental and Behavioral Pediatrics, 29,* 475–82.

Forehand, R., & Scarboro, M. E. (1975). An analysis of children's oppositional behavior. *Journal of Abnormal Child Psychology, 3,* 27–31.

Frey, K. S., Hirschstein, M. K., & Guzzo, B. A. (2000). Second Step: Preventing aggression by promoting social competence. *Journal of Emotional and Behavioral Disorders, 8,* 102–12.

Frodi, A. M., & Lamb, M. E. (1980). Child abusers' responses to infant smiles and cries. *Child Development, 51*, 238.

Garner, P. W. (2006). Prediction of prosocial and emotional competence from maternal behavior in African American preschoolers. *Cultural Diversity & Ethnic Minority Psychology, 12*, 179–98.

Gartrell, D. (2001). Replacing time-out: Part one—Using guidance to build an encouraging classroom. *Young Children*, (November), 8–16.

Greenhill, L., Kollins, S., Abikoff, H., McCracken, J., Riddle, M., Swanson, J.,…Cooper, T. (2006). Efficacy and safety of immediate-release methylphenidate treatment for preschoolers with ADHD. *Journal of the American Academy of Child and Adolescent Psychiatry, 45*(11), 1284–93.

Halberstadt, A. G. (1991). Toward an ecology of expressiveness: Family socialization in particular and a model in general. In R. S. Feldman & B. Rime (Eds.), *Fundamentals of nonverbal behavior* (pp. 106–60). Cambridge University Press.

Hamlet, C. C., Axelrod, S., & Kuerschner, S. (1984). Eye contact as an antecedent to compliant behavior. *Journal of Applied Behavior Analysis, 17*(4), 553–7. Retrieved from http://www.pubmedcentral.nih.gov/articlerender.fcgi?artid=1307977&tool=pmcentrez&rendertype=abstract.

Hammond, S. I., Müller, U., Carpendale, J. I. M., Bibok, M. B., & Liebermann-Finestone, D. P. (2012). The effects of parental scaffolding on preschoolers' executive function. *Developmental Psychology, 48*, 271–81.

Harvey, E. A., Friedman-Weieneth, J. L., Goldstein, L. H., & Sherman, A. H. (2007). Examining subtypes of behavior problems among 3-year-old children, Part I: Investigating validity of subtypes and biological risk-factors. *Journal of Abnormal Child Psychology, 35*, 97–110.

Harvey, E. A., Youngwirth, S. D., Thakar, D. A., & Errazuriz, P. A. (2009). Predicting attention-deficit/hyperactivity disorder and oppositional defiant disorder from preschool diagnostic assessments. *Journal of Consulting and Clinical Psychology, 77*, 349–54.

Henderlong, J., & Lepper, M. R. (2002). The effects of praise on children's intrinsic motivation: A review and synthesis. *Psychological Bulletin, 128*, 774–95.

Herbert, S. D., Harvey, E.A., Roberts, J. L., Wichowski, K., & Lugo-Candelas, C. I. (2013). A randomized controlled trial of a parent training and emotion socialization program for families of hyperactive preschool-aged children. *Behavior Therapy, 44*(2), 302–16.

Herbert, S. D., Harvey, E. H., & Halgin, R. P. (2014). The balancing act—ethical issues in parent training research: Confidentiality, harm reduction, and methodology. *Ethics & Behavior*. Advance Online Publication.

Herschell, A. D., Calzada, E. J., Eyberg, S. M., & McNeil, C. B. (2002). Parent-child interaction therapy: New directions in research. *Cognitive and Behavioral Practice, 9*, 9–16.

Houlihan, D., & Jones, R. N. (1990). Exploring the reinforcement of compliance with "do" and "don't" requests and the side effects: a partial replication and extension. *Psychological Reports, 67*, 439–48.

Huang, H.-L., Chao, C.-C., Tu, C.-C., & Yang, P.-C. (2003). Behavioral parent training for Taiwanese parents of children with attention-deficit/hyperactivity disorder. *Psychiatry and Clinical Neurosciences, 57*(3), 275–81.

Johnston, C., & Mash, E. J. (2001). Families of children with attention-deficit / hyperactivity disorder : Review and recommendations for future research. *Clinical Child and Family Psychology Review, 4*(3), 183–207. Retrieved from http://www.ncbi.nlm.nih.gov/pubmed/11783738.

Jones, K., Daley, D., Hutchings, J., Bywater, T., & Eames, C. (2008). Efficacy of the Incredible Years Programme as an early intervention for children with conduct problems and ADHD: Long-term follow-up. *Child: Care, Health and Development, 34*(3), 380–90.

Keenan, K., Wakschlag, L. S., & Danis, B. (2001). *Kiddie-Disruptive Behavior Disorder Schedule (version 1.1).*

Kern, L., DuPaul, G. J., Volpe, R. J., Sokol, N. G., Lutz, J. G., Arbolino, L. A.,... VanBrakle, J. D. (2007). Multisetting assessment-based intervention for young children at risk for attention deficit hyperactivity disorder: Initial effects on academic and behavioral functioning. *School Psychology Review, 36*(2), 237–54.

Klimes-Dougan, B., & Kopp, C. B. (1999). Children's conflict tactics with mothers : A longitudinal investigation of the toddler and preschool years. *Merrill-Palmer Quarterly, 45*, 226–41.

Kochanska, G., Forman, D. R., Aksan, N., & Dunbar, S. B. (2005). Pathways to conscience: Early mother-child mutually responsive orientation and children's moral emotion, conduct, and cognition. *Journal of Child Psychology and Psychiatry, and Allied Disciplines, 46*, 19–34.

Kohls, G., Herpertz-Dahlmann, B., & Konrad, K. (2009). Hyperresponsiveness to social rewards in children and adolescents with attention-deficit/hyperactivity disorder (ADHD). *Behavioral and Brain Functions, 5*, 20.

Kollins, S., Greenhill, L., Swanson, J., Wigal, S., Abikoff, H., McCracken, J.,... Bauzo, A. (2006). Rationale, design, and methods of the Preschool ADHD Treatment Study (PATS). *Journal of the American Academy of Child and Adolescent Psychiatry, 45*(11), 1275–83.

Lahey, B. B., Pelham, W. E., Loney, J., Lee, S. S., & Willcutt, E. (2005). Instability of the DSM-IV subtypes of ADHD from preschool through elementary school. *Archives of General Psychiatry, 62*, 896–902.

Lewis, M. (2008). The emergence of human emotions. *Handbook of Emotions (3rd Ed.)* (pp. 304–19). New York, NY: Guilford Press.

Little, L. M., & Kelley, M. Lou. (1989). The efficacy of response cost procedures for reducing children's noncompliance to parental instructions. *Behavior Therapy, 20*(4), 525–34.

Lyubomirsky, S., King, L., & Diener, E. (2005). The benefits of frequent positive affect: does happiness lead to success? *Psychological Bulletin, 131*, 803–55.

Martel, M. M. (2009). Research review: A new perspective on attention-deficit/hyperactivity disorder: Emotion dysregulation and trait models. *Journal of Child Psychology and Psychiatry, and Allied Disciplines, 50*, 1042–51.

Matos, M., Bauermeister, J. J., & Bernal, G. (2009). Parent-Child Interaction Therapy for Puerto Rican preschool children with ADHD and behavior problems: A pilot efficacy study. *Family Process, 48*, 232–52.

Matthys, W., Cuperus, J. M., & Van Engeland, H. (1999). Deficient social problem-solving in boys with ODD/CD, with ADHD, and with both disorders. *Journal of the American Academy of Child & Adolescent Psychiatry, 38*, 311–21.

Morawska, A., & Sanders, M. (2010). Parental use of time out revisited: A useful or harmful parenting strategy? *Journal of Child and Family Studies, 20*, 1–8.

Nelson, C. A., & Bloom, F. E. (1997). Child development and neuroscience. *Child Development, 68*, 970–87.

Normand, S., Schneider, B. H., Lee, M. D., Maisonneuve, M. F., Chupetlovska-Anastasova, A., Kuehn, S. M., & Robaey, P. (2013). Continuities and changes in the friendships of children with and without ADHD: A longitudinal, observational study. *Journal of Abnormal Child Psychology, 41*, 1161–75.

Owen, D. J., Slep, A. M. S., & Heyman, R. E. (2012). The effect of praise, positive nonverbal response, reprimand, and negative nonverbal response on child compliance: A systematic review. *Clinical Child and Family Psychology Review, 15*, 364–85.

Owen, D. J., Smith Slep, A. M., & Heyman, R. E. (2009). The association of promised consequences with child compliance to maternal directives. *Journal of Clinical Child and Adolescent Psychology, 38*, 639–49.

Patterson, G. R. (2002). The early development of coercive family process. In J. B. Reid, G. R. Patterson, & J. Snyder (Eds.), *Antisocial behavior in children and adolescents: A developmental analysis and model for intervention* (pp. 25–44). Washington, DC, US: American Psychological Association.

Pisterman, S., Firestone, P., McGrath, P., Goodman, J. T., Webster, I., Mallory, R., & Goffin, B. (1992). The role of parent training in treatment of preschoolers with ADDH. *American Journal of Orthopsychiatry, 62*(3), 397–408.

Pisterman, S., McGrath, P. J., Firestone, P., & Goodman, J. T. (1989). Outcome of parent-mediated treatment of preschoolers with attention deficit disorder with hyperactivity. *Journal of Consulting and Clinical Psychology, 57*(5), 628–35.

Raikes, H. A., Virmani, E. A., Thompson, R. A., & Hatton, H. (2013). Declines in peer conflict from preschool through first grade: Influences from early attachment and social information processing. *Attachment & Human Development, 15*, 65–82.

Rajwan, E., Chacko, A., & Moeller, M. (2012). Nonpharmacological interventions for preschool ADHD: State of the evidence and implications for practice. *Professional Psychology: Research and Practice, 43*(5), 520–6.

Reid, M. J., Webster-Stratton, C., & Baydar, N. (2004). Halting the development of conduct problems in Head Start children: The effects of parent training. *Journal of Clinical Child & Adolescent Psychology, 33*(2), 279–91.

Riddle, M. A., Yershova, K., Lazzaretto, D., Paykina, N., Yenokyan, G., Greenhill, L., . . . Posner, K. (2013). The preschool attention-deficit/hyperactivity disorder treatment study (PATS) 6-year follow-up. *Journal of the American Academy of Child and Adolescent Psychiatry, 52*, 264–78.e2.

Roberts, M. W., McMahon, R. J., Forehand, R., & Humphreys, L. (1978). The effect of parental instruction-giving on child compliance. *Behavior Therapy, 9*, 793–8.

Robertson, C. D., Kimbrel, N. A., & Nelson-Gray, R. O. (2013). The Invalidating Childhood Environment Scale (ICES): Psychometric properties and relationship to borderline personality symptomatology. *Journal of Personality Disorders, 27*, 402–10.

Rosen, L. A., O'Leary, S. G., Joyce, S. A., Conway, G., & Pfiffner, L. J. (1984). The importance of prudent negative consequences for maintaining the appropriate behavior of hyperactive students. *Journal of Abnormal Child Psychology, 12*, 581–604.

Shaw, D. S., Lacourse, E., & Nagin, D. S. (2005). Developmental trajectories of conduct problems and hyperactivity from ages 2 to 10. *Journal of Child Psychology and Psychiatry, and Allied Disciplines, 46*, 931–42.

Shenk, C. E., & Fruzzetti, A. E. (2011). The impact of validating and invalidating responses on emotional reactivity. *Journal of Social and Clinical Psychology, 30*, 163–83.

Shin, N., Vaughn, B. E., Akers, V., Kim, M., Stevens, S., Krzysik, L.,...Korth, B. (2011). Are happy children socially successful? Testing a central premise of positive psychology in a sample of preschool children. *The Journal of Positive Psychology, 6,* 355–67.

Sinzig, J., Morsch, D., & Lehmkuhl, G. (2008). Do hyperactivity, impulsivity and inattention have an impact on the ability of facial affect recognition in children with autism and ADHD? *European Child & Adolescent Psychiatry, 17,* 63–72.

Skinner, B. F. (1974). *About behaviorism.* Oxford, England: Alfred A. Knopf.

Snyder, C. R., Hoza, B., Pelham, W. E., Rapoff, M., Ware, L., Danovsky, M.,...Stahl, K. J. (1997). The development and validation of the Children's Hope Scale. *Journal of Pediatric Psychology, 22,* 399–421.

Sonuga-Barke, E. J., Daley, D., Thompson, M., Laver-Bradbury, C., & Weeks, A. (2001). Parent-based therapies for preschool attention-deficit/hyperactivity disorder: A randomized, controlled trial with a community sample. *Journal of the American Academy of Child and Adolescent Psychiatry, 40*(4), 402–8.

Strayhorn, J. M., & Weidman, C. S. (1989). Reduction of attention deficit and internalizing symptoms in preschoolers through parent-child interaction training. *Journal of the American Academy of Child and Adolescent Psychiatry, 28*(6), 888–96.

Strayhorn, J. M., & Weidman, C. S. (1991). Follow-up one year after parent-child interaction training: effects on behavior of preschool children. *Journal of the American Academy of Child and Adolescent Psychiatry, 30*(1), 138–43.

Subcommittee on Attention-Deficit/Hyperactivity Disorder Committee on Quality. (2011). ADHD: Clinical practice guideline for the diagnosis, evaluation, and treatment of attention-deficit/hyperactivity disorder in children and adolescents. *Pediatrics, 128*(5), 1007–22.

Supplee, L. H., Skuban, E. M., Trentacosta, C. J., Shaw, D. S., & Stoltz, E. (2011). Preschool boys' development of emotional self-regulation strategies in a sample at risk for behavior problems. *The Journal of Genetic Psychology, 172,* 95–120.

Swanson, J. M., Elliott, G. R., Greenhill, L. L., Wigal, T., Arnold, L. E., Vitiello, B.,...Volkow, N. D. (2007). Effects of stimulant medication on growth rates across 3 years in the MTA follow-up. *Journal of the American Academy of Child and Adolescent Psychiatry, 46*(8), 1015–27.

The MTA Cooperative Group. (1999). A 14-month randomized clinical trial of treatment strategies for attention-deficit/hyperactivity disorder. *Archives of General Psychiatry, 56,* 1073–86.

Thompson, M. J. J., Laver-Bradbury, C., Ayres, M., Le Poidevin, E., Mead, S., Dodds, C.,...Sonuga-Barke, E. J. S. (2009). A small-scale randomized controlled trial of the revised new forest parenting programme for preschoolers with attention deficit hyperactivity disorder. *European Child & Adolescent Psychiatry, 18*(10), 605–16.

Tottenham, N. (2012). Human amygdala development in the absence of species-expected caregiving. *Developmental Psychobiology, 54,* 598–611.

Visser, S. N., Danielson, M. L., Bitsko, R. H., Holbrook, J. R., Kogan, M. D., Ghandour, R. M.,...Blumberg, S. J. (2014). Trends in the parent-report of health care provider-diagnosed and medicated attention-deficit/hyperactivity disorder: United States, 2003-2011. *Journal of the American Academy of Child and Adolescent Psychiatry, 53*(1), 34–46.e2.

Vygotsky, L. S. (1978). *Mind in society: The development of higher psychological process.* Cambridge, MA: Harvard University Press.

Wakschlag, L. S., Choi, S. W., Carter, A. S., Hullsiek, H., Burns, J., McCarthy, K.,...Briggs-Gowan, M. J. (2012). Defining the developmental parameters of temper loss in early childhood: Implications for developmental psychopathology. *Journal of Child Psychology and Psychiatry, and Allied Disciplines, 53*, 1099–108.

Walcott, C. M., & Landau, S. (2004). The relation between disinhibition and emotion regulation in boys with attention deficit hyperactivity disorder. *Journal of Clinical Child and Adolescent Psychology, 33*, 772–82.

Webster-Stratton, C. H., Reid, J., & Hammond, M. (2001). Social skills and problem-solving training for children with early-onset conduct problems: Who benefits? *Journal of Child Psychology and Psychiatry, and Allied Disciplines, 42*, 943–52.

Webster-Stratton, C. H., Reid, M. J., & Beauchaine, T. (2011). Combining parent and child training for young children with ADHD. *Journal of Clinical Child and Adolescent Psychology, 40*, 191–203.

Weissbourd, R. (2009). Why are we praising our children so much? *Psychology Today.* Retrieved from http://www.psychologytoday.com/blog/the-parents-we-mean-be/200904/why-are-we-praising-our-children-so-much.

Wigal, T., Greenhill, L., Chuang, S., McGough, J., Vitiello, B., Skrobala, A.,...Stehli, A. (2006). Safety and tolerability of methylphenidate in preschool children with ADHD. *Journal of the American Academy of Child and Adolescent Psychiatry, 45*(11), 1294–303.

Williams, L. M., Hermens, D. F., Palmer, D., Kohn, M., Clarke, S., Keage, H.,...Gordon, E. (2008). Misinterpreting emotional expressions in attention-deficit/hyperactivity disorder: evidence for a neural marker and stimulant effects. *Biological Psychiatry, 63*, 917–26.

Wood, D., Bruner, J. S., & Ross, G. (1976). The role of tutoring in problem-solving. *Journal of Child Psychology and Psychiatry, 17*, 89–100.

Yeates, K. O., Schultz, L. H., & Selman, R. L. (1991). The development of interpersonal negotiation strategies in thought and action: A social-cognitive link to behavioral adjustment and social status. *Merrill-Palmer Quarterly, 37*, 368–405.

Zito, J. M., Safer, D. J., DosReis, S., Gardner, J. F., Boles, M., & Lynch, F. (2000). Trends in the prescribing of psychotropic medications to preschoolers. *Journal of the American Medical Association, 283*(8), 1025–30.

Elizabeth A. Harvey, PhD, is currently a professor in the psychology department at the University of Massachusetts Amherst and a licensed psychologist. She earned her PhD in clinical psychology from Stony Brook University in 1995. Dr. Harvey has spent the past two decades conducting research to advance our understanding of the early development of ADHD and related behavior problems in children.

Sharonne D. Herbert, PhD, is a licensed psychologist in the Pediatric Psychology Department at Children's Hospital of Orange County. She earned her PhD in clinical psychology from the University of Massachusetts Amherst in 2013. Dr. Herbert is an early-career psychologist who conducted applied research for families of hyperactive preschoolers in graduate school.

Rebecca M. Stowe, PhD, is currently a lecturer in the psychology department at the University of Massachusetts Amherst and a licensed psychologist. She is a clinical supervisor and senior clinician in the UMass Psychological Services Center. She earned her PhD in clinical psychology from the University of Massachusetts Amherst in 1999. Dr. Stowe's clinical interests include parenting and young children with behavioral difficulties and ADHD.